KRISTOPHER J. N

T0290064

Aligning
Instructional
Design

With
Business
Goals

Make the Case and Deliver Results

PRESS

ALEXANDRIA, VA

ATD Press is an internationally renowned source of insightful and practical information on talent development, training, and professional development.

ATD Press
1640 King Street
Alexandria, VA 22314 USA

Ordering information: Books published by ATD Press can be purchased by visiting ATD's website at td.org/books or by calling 800.628.2783 or 703.683.8100.

Library of Congress Control Number: 2023934777

ISBN-10: 1-953946-57-7
ISBN-13: 978-1-953946-57-7
e-ISBN: 978-1-957157-40-5

ATD Press Editorial Staff
Director: Sarah Halgas
Manager: Melissa Jones
Content Manager, Learning & Development: Jes Thompson
Developmental Editor: Alexandra Andrzejewski
Production Editor: Katy Wiley Stewts
Text Designer: Shirley E.M. Raybuck
Cover Designer: Rose Richey

Printed by BR Printers, San Jose, CA

*To everyone I've had the pleasure
of learning from and teaching over the years.
You've all inspired this book and helped me
become a better learner, teacher, and person.*

*And especially to my mom and dad,
who have always encouraged me to be me
and to always pursue my dreams.*

Contents

Foreword

Not everyone enters the talent development (TD) profession with a relevant undergraduate or graduate degree. Rather, they end up in talent development by happenstance—many are promoted from within their organizations to help launch organized training, organization development, career development, or the myriad other activities generally covered under the banner of talent development. Some people who are promoted into talent development pursue professional certifications in the field, such as the Association for Talent Development's Certified Professional in Talent Development (CPTD).

But the need remains to give newcomers to the field—and even some old-timers in the field who never got a proper orientation—a broad-brush introduction to the profession, what it seeks to accomplish, how it should be positioned in an organization, and how it should identify and pursue its purpose.

This book provides a solid foundation to review what the talent development profession is, how to align talent development in the organization with business needs, how to build support for it in organizations, and how to carry out the most important activities traditionally handed to the talent development function.

This book is the primer I wish I'd had when I began my own career in talent development as a trainer for the state of Illinois in 1979, before later moving on to manage talent development in a large insurance company. By stimulating meaningful self-reflection, it will help my many students who are starting out or at midcareer and are reflecting on what they want to do.

I met Kris through our mutual work with the International Accreditors for Continuing Education and Training (IACET), the successor organization to the U.S. Department of Education task force that developed the continuing education unit. Accreditation is key for ensuring quality organizational talent development efforts and programs, and Kris has been a leader in that organization; he served as the chair of the organization's board of directors while writing this book. Kris has also been involved with research projects sponsored by IACET in partnership with ATD on instructional design and evaluation, and we have both spoken at numerous ATD conferences, together and separately.

Kris has done an outstanding job of providing a practical primer for talent development professionals who need to hit the ground running in an increasingly demanding field where skilling, reskilling, and upskilling workers are challenges facing organizations and nations. I highly recommend this book to anyone who works in talent development.

—William J. Rothwell, PhD, DBA, SPHR, SHRM-SCP, CPTD Fellow,
President, Rothwell & Associates; Distinguished Professor, Workforce
Education and Development, The Pennsylvania State University

Introduction

To design great learning programs, you need to focus on the desired impact on your company. To home in on impact, you need to speak the language of business. And to speak the language of business, you need to speak the language of money. That's right—it's all about the money.

The good news is that reframing the work you do to put out valuable instructional design content can be accomplished with a few concrete steps—not at the expense of the people you entered this profession to serve in the first place.

Consider this example: A graduate student of mine several years ago worked as the principal of a local public school. As part of an assignment in their graduate course on measurement and evaluation in HR development, the students were required to reframe a course's purpose statement into a business goal to evaluate the impact of a talent development (TD) initiative. This student initially rejected the challenge, suggesting it was impossible to get to the language of business—*money*—in the realm of public education.

My challenge, of course, was to help her get there, even for a not-for-profit municipal school. After all, every legitimate organization requires financial viability to exist, whether it relies on donations, government funding, or profits. So, we must accept that it's possible to reframe course purpose statements as real business goals. Thomas Gilbert, a psychologist who founded the field of human performance technology, postulated that virtually everything can be measured. He suggested that we focus on worthy accomplishments rather than behaviors that lead to them. That is precisely what I suggested to her, and what I suggest you do with respect to the curriculum you design.

To assist my student in getting down to the money, I posed a question—the first why of several: "Why is it important that teachers *can* prepare students for standardized testing?"

"*Why* is *that* important?" she replied, as if I had just asked the most absurd question.

"Yes, why is it important for teachers to prepare students for standardized testing?" I asked.

She said, "Our students' standardized test scores have declined over the past couple years, and they need to improve. That's why the teacher training program is so important. It's meant to better prepare teachers to ensure students are prepared for and can pass state tests."

"OK, good," I said. Now for the second why; I asked, "So why is improving standardized test scores important?" Again, I was met with a look that suggested I should just inherently know why, but I wanted her to be able to articulate it so she could see that she was capable of getting to the business goal related to money, even for a public school.

"Because we're getting bad press over it," she said. "The school's reputation is being called into question. As a result, parents are taking their kids out and transferring them to other schools. And good teachers are leaving to go work for schools with higher test scores."

We were getting closer. Now for the third why; I asked, "Why is losing students and teachers a bad thing for the school?"

"Because our state funding is dependent upon the number of students who actively attend the school! The more teachers we lose, the more students we lose. The more students we lose, the more money we—OK, *now* I see where you are going with this!"

Aha! In just three "whys," we reframed the course purpose statement into a business goal using the language of business. Consider the difference between *demonstrating a change in teacher behavior* (the original course goal) and *committing to an increase in state funding, thereby increasing the school's revenue*, because of the program. Which argument do you think is more compelling to a school superintendent? This exercise applies to both public education and corporate learning, and across industries to all types of TD initiatives. What this book will do is help you go from communicating your TD-focused objectives to communicating ones that matter and are compelling to your stakeholders.

The Importance of Stakeholders

I want to stress how transformative it can be for you to keep the end goal in mind (the money), collaborate with your stakeholders to arrive there, and tailor your impact to those who matter most. An important lesson I learned in my career was how to identify, prioritize, and engage stakeholders in establishing and agreeing upon evaluation criteria that will be used to inform successful instructional design content.

I completed an undergraduate degree in secondary education and spent a brief time teaching at two high schools in western Michigan before eventually landing a corporate job in employee training and development. When I took my first HR role as a training specialist on a training team, I had no formal experience in training adults. However, I felt absolutely comfortable designing curriculum because I had regularly designed lesson plans that explicitly aligned to state curriculum standards.

In both experiences, though, I wondered if instructional design alone was the best measure of my success as a teacher and subsequently as a training specialist. Was it sufficient to simply know I had designed, developed, and implemented curriculum that satisfied established education standards? How *should* I evaluate my own success as a teacher? That was my first real personal inquiry into measurement and evaluation.

I found myself attempting to evaluate my teaching performance from several perspectives: how students might evaluate me, how parents might evaluate me, how school administrators might evaluate me, how community employers might evaluate me, and how I might evaluate myself. It grew increasingly clear to me that a plethora of stakeholders had a vested interest in my performance as a teacher. All of these stakeholders were important, but was one more important than the others? Was one dependent upon another? How would I balance competing expectations from various stakeholders? How would I manage the expectations of all stakeholders, knowing I couldn't possibly satisfy everyone equally? This is one of my first recollections of having to identify stakeholders and understand their interests in and influence over my work. As with any evaluation, it highlighted the need to understand not only who the various stakeholders were, but also their expectations of a successful teacher and the evaluation criteria they might use to determine it.

From the students' perspectives, likability and relatability were clear requirements, but these were merely student *reactions* to me as a person—Level 1 of the five levels of evaluation framework (which I discuss in chapter 6)—not necessarily measures of how effective I was as a teacher. Having once been a high-school student, I understood that they wanted to feel respected, to be set up for success, and to feel like they mattered. Being only a few years older than the students I was teaching at the time, I decided to ignore the school's faculty dress code and instead wore jeans to class every day. My jeans and T-shirts may not have been deemed professional or even appropriate by school administrators, other teachers, parents, or community taxpayers, but dressing like my students helped remove an unnecessary barrier between us. Although their reactions to me would not determine how successful I was, I understood that if I couldn't even get them to *react* or respond to me, I would have even more difficulty getting them to *learn*. The lesson for me was not to discount the importance of students as stakeholders, even if their primary measures of success for me were their reactions, and even if earning their favorable reactions meant breaking long-standing rules.

In addition to adapting how I dressed, I also quickly understood that I needed to speak their language. So, at the beginning of each class, I devoted time for students to teach me their contemporary slang. They invited me into their subculture by sharing their language, which helped me understand what they were talking about and helped me speak in a way that connected to their interests. This is one of the most important lessons I learned, and it's one of the most important pieces of advice I offer to others now: Learn to speak the language of the audience with whom you're attempting to build rapport and credibility.

Learn to speak the language of the audience with whom you're attempting to build rapport and credibility.

It also dawned on me that aligning the course curriculum with state education standards and measuring learning through test scores alone wouldn't be sufficient. A real measure of my effectiveness and success transcended how much learning occurred in the classroom. I needed to prepare students for real-world application, so in my civics class, I invested in helping them become law-abiding, well-informed members of society who understood due process and the rule of law.

Since my days of teaching in a high-school classroom, I've acquired formal education in and experience with adult learning. I completed two graduate degrees in HR: one in HR management (traditional HR) and one in HR development (another way of saying *talent development*). I have earned and maintain several professional credentials in HR, talent development, and performance improvement. Even so, the lessons I learned in those high-school classrooms—identifying stakeholders, understanding their expectations, and doing everything I could to win over their hearts and minds and change their behaviors—continue to have tremendous implications for my career and life. This book will teach you how to do the same with your stakeholders. Learning to attend to the motives and expectations of all of your stakeholder groups can prepare you to make the case and deliver results.

The Making of a Book

The idea for this book was inspired by the same graduate course I discussed in the opening story. When I reviewed the business challenges my graduate students were attempting to address through their instructional design packages, I found them to be incomplete. Rationales such as "reduce turnover," "reduce errors," or "teach *XYZ* skills" without ever getting to *why* they are important will not consistently lead to effective results. That's when I realized that I needed to help others think like business leaders and understand the importance of establishing evaluation criteria up front that would inform their instructional design.

My wish for my students is my wish for you: If I can help you understand how to design and develop TD initiatives that achieve explicit, mutually agreeable business goals, you will:

- Create stronger, more effective instructional design packages.
- Understand the business you support.
- Demonstrate the value you add to the business.
- Be recognized as critical to business success.

This book will be particularly relevant for the following TD professionals:

- **Instructional designers and individual contributors.** This is primarily a book focused on rethinking the way TD professionals design instruction using evaluation. It helps you consider what knowledge, skills, and attitudes are necessary for achieving business goals, and it provides strategies for measurement and evaluation that help prove meaningful learning. Although this book isn't a measurement and evaluation text, it can help enhance partnerships between measurement and evaluation specialists, instructional designers, and business leaders.

- **TD leaders.** Although, practically speaking, this book funnels its strategies into instructional design, it also encourages talent development leaders to collaborate with business leaders and reimagine the TD function to ensure that learning is aligned with business goals. It offers ideas for restructuring your learning portfolio, exploring business needs and whether learning is appropriate to address them, aligning with various stakeholder groups, and measuring the output of your function to add the most value possible to your enterprise.

Everything I do in talent development relies upon understanding the business I serve and speaking the language of business. TD professionals who understand business goals will design, develop, and implement more meaningful TD initiatives when they keep evaluation in mind. The processes and tools I use to accomplish meaningful learning programs that add real value and deliver results have made my professional life both easier and more successful, and I am confident they will work for you, too.

In This Book

This book is organized into two parts that encourage TD professionals to use measurement and evaluation techniques to inform their instructional design content.

The first part of the book, "Foundations for Making Your Case," discusses how you can develop business acumen, align with your business leaders, and make your case as a valuable, integrated part of business success.

Chapter 1 approaches talent development as a critical business development partner. It explores how TD initiatives are intended to change behaviors that produce necessary business results, and offers a model for changing peoples' behaviors to produce those results. It explores an updated version of ADDIE that prioritizes evaluation criteria to inform learning objectives.

Chapter 2 focuses on identifying, prioritizing, and engaging your stakeholders to ensure maximum success. It offers several approaches to conducting stakeholder analyses.

Chapter 3 considers how to get buy-in for your TD initiatives. It proposes a new or reimagined TD function that's better positioned to produce meaningful initiatives.

Chapter 4 focuses on building business acumen. It addresses the language of business as a way to build rapport and establish greater credibility with business leaders. It approaches course goals from the perspective of business results to change the way learners think and feel about talent development. It differentiates between *outputs* and *outcomes* in ways that help you identify the real value your initiatives add to the business.

The second part of the book, "The Eight-Step Evaluation-Focused Instructional Design Framework," explores how to better align your initiatives with the business. The framework's eight steps emphasize the importance of collaborating with business leaders and other stakeholders in everything you do to maximize the value you add and to be seen as essential to the success of the business.

Chapter 5 walks through the first two steps: Identify a business challenge and translate the business challenges into a business goal. These steps focus on conducting a needs analysis and establishing evaluation criteria. Proactively identifying business needs, understanding root causes, and closing performance gaps are all considered.

Chapter 6 covers the next two steps: Determine if learning is an appropriate strategy for achieving a goal and determine what successful learning looks like. Both focus on establishing evaluation criteria that are used to inform your instructional design content. This chapter uses the five levels of evaluation as the framework for evaluation criteria.

Chapter 7 covers the remaining steps of the process: Determine what knowledge is needed to achieve the business goal, determine what skills are needed to achieve the goal, use needed knowledge and skills to inform course objectives, and, for each course objective, design and develop learning activities. These steps are all geared toward finally designing and developing your learning initiative. This chapter addresses determining the knowledge and skills necessary to change learners' behaviors to produce results, identifying course learning objectives, and designing course activities intended for learners to demonstrate their proficiency.

I hope you can engage with the content in this book as action learning by applying the process I share to a real challenge facing your business. I want to empower you to define evaluation criteria that inform initiatives that contribute to your business's success.

PART 1

FOUNDATIONS FOR MAKING YOUR CASE

The first part of this book focuses on how you can position your TD function for success. It's vital that you understand the business you serve as well as you understand talent development. When you demonstrate your understanding of and commitment to your company's core competencies, you build credibility and trust with business leaders. Learn how you can contribute to real business results by intentionally changing behaviors—something you're already in the business of doing. Also explore how identifying, categorizing, prioritizing, and engaging stakeholders is critical to the success of your initiatives.

Chapter 1
Talent Development as Business Development

I used to consider myself an educator, not a businessperson. I didn't study business. I didn't have a desire to lead or own a business. I wasn't motivated by money or the prospect of getting rich working in business. I found peace and comfort in thinking and feeling that being an educator was a more noble, selfless occupation—one that existed to make a difference in the lives of others for the betterment of society and humankind. That is how I thought and what I felt . . . and it was fulfilling! However, I have since come to recognize the importance of being business-minded by changing how I think about the role of money, which changes how I feel about the role of talent development as a *business* function—not just a *people* function—which changes how I approach my work as a TD professional.

A basic premise of this book is that TD professionals still must convince business leaders of the value talent development adds, and that is because in many companies and organizations talent development is still not considered part of *the business*. Rather, it's often considered a support or enablement function, along with IT, finance, legal, and HR. Over the years, as talent development grew into its own established profession, that evolution may have perpetuated the divide. Although establishing talent development as a distinct profession has, in many ways, legitimized our place in the world of work, it may have also resulted in our work being perceived by those in the business as *nice to have* rather than *essential*. Because we're not always seen as part of *the business*, we're not always included in addressing business problems or opportunities, such as how to fix declining revenue or expand into new markets. However, by homing in on the goals of your business, applying what you already know about behavior change, and rethinking the process you use to launch TD initiatives, you can become essential to the business you support.

A Case Study in Retail and Revenue

While working on my secondary education degree, I managed a Harry & David store, an upscale gourmet food and gift retailer, on Chicago's Michigan Avenue—the "Magnificent Mile." When I took over the store, it was a total mess. It was understaffed. Absenteeism was a regular occurrence. There was more inventory in the stockroom than on the sales floor. Signage was outdated and incorrect. There had been very little upkeep. As I trained the staff and worked with them to turn the store around (we began to regularly appear on the list of top-performing stores in the region), I started to understand that *it's all about the money.*

Nothing had changed about our products, price points, foot traffic, location, advertising, or marketing. (Although, we were literally spending hours before opening and after closing each day on our hands and knees cleaning the floors and fixtures and making the store bright, clean, and fun!) I admitted to corporate executives that I wasn't focused on increasing revenue, which was a naive, albeit honest, sentiment. Rather, I took over the store with an intrinsic desire to assemble a team of engaged colleagues who cared about our collective success and had fun doing the job, make the best of my time there by building rapport with customers, and walk out at the end of each day feeling accomplished and proud. I wasn't there to sell products, but engaging and empowering staff resulted in customers spending more money. So, there seemed to be a collateral benefit to this approach.

I hired new sales associates and reengaged the existing staff. I convinced the team to join me in creating a great experience for everyone, and they rose to the occasion. None of us were focused on revenue, yet our sales continued to grow and grow. The more revenue the store brought in, the more payroll budget I had available to offer employees more hours. The more hours my colleagues could work, the more our store improved and the more potential they had for taking home more money. The more we continued to improve and the more they worked, the more I was able to increase their pay. It was all interconnected. When we improved one thing, it influenced another, and the outcome of our work reinforced our behaviors.

So what happened to turn that store around? I focused on the people: *employees* and *customers*. These were the stakeholders I was determined to prioritize and engage. And when I did, the money followed.

When I began working at Rotary International on its TD team, my role wasn't revenue oriented or focused on money. I struggled because when I left the office each day, I had no real way to know or measure the impact I was making. This was a sharp contrast to working in retail, when not a day went by that I didn't know how the store was performing from a sales perspective. I had learned from retail that the better a company or organization performs financially, the better the conditions can be for the people—the *stakeholders*. It suddenly clicked how important being business minded was. I realized that if I wanted to continue to care about making a difference in the lives of others, I needed to become an astute businessperson.

If you came to the profession wanting to make a difference in the lives of others, then the best way to do that is acting like a businessperson first and a TD professional second. If, like me, you have very little interest in participating in the profit-generating arm of your organization, I hope to make a case to you that your professional life will be easier and more fulfilling if you can change the way you think and feel about money when it comes to producing instructional design content.

Making Your Case

Each year, companies and organizations around the world invest billions of dollars in TD initiatives for their employees, customers, members, and volunteers. The purpose of these initiatives is for learners to acquire, maintain, or improve competencies with the express intention of changing their behaviors to achieve a desired business strategy.

Unfortunately, some business leaders view and treat the TD function or TD initiatives as expenses—*cost centers*—rather than as investments. This can be a tremendous source of frustration for us. How do we get business leaders to consider our activities necessary investments? How do we convince them that such activities are essential to helping the business achieve desired results?

The mere fact that we struggle with the answers to these questions highlights an important reality: We often approach this dilemma from an us-versus-them perspective. How do *we* get *them* to recognize the importance of TD activities? How do *we* get *them* to view TD activities as investments rather than expenses? This conflict suggests that business leaders might not fully appreciate talent development, and that practitioners may not fully understand the business. It presents an opportunity for us to be perceived by business leaders as *business partners.*

To establish credibility with business leaders and have talent development seen as a legitimate discipline in business management, it's imperative to reconsider the role of measurement and evaluation in your work. One of the challenges for the TD profession is that evaluating a training program's impact is often an afterthought, considered only after training has been conducted, or it gets overlooked altogether (even though evaluating the impact of TD initiatives is a core part of ATD's Talent Development Capability Model). For business leaders who are accustomed to relying upon metrics that measure the success and failure of business initiatives, the usual TD metrics (such as the number of training courses offered and the number of learners who completed courses) are insufficient. They're measures of output, not outcomes. The most powerful metrics are those that help us understand impact. As TD professionals, we need to ensure we're skilled at measuring what matters and use evaluation data to tell the story of the value we add.

As TD professionals, we need to ensure we're skilled at measuring what matters and use evaluation data to tell the story of the value we add.

In my experience working with hundreds of TD graduate students, it's clear that measurement and evaluation is perceived as the least glamorous TD activity for a lot of practitioners, and many avoid it completely. I would argue, though, that it's one of the most critical activities to ensuring that everything else you do (designing, developing, and delivering initiatives) makes a difference in the success of the business you support.

One way to promote measurement and evaluation is to position it as critical to instructional design. Doing so renders it essential rather than optional. The following eight-step Evaluation-Focused Instructional Design Framework does just that and will be the focus of part 2 of this book:

1. Identify a business challenge.
2. Translate the challenge into a business goal.
3. Determine if learning is an appropriate strategy for achieving the business goal.
4. Determine what successful learning looks like using four of the five levels of evaluation.
5. Determine what knowledge is needed to achieve the business goal.
6. Determine what skills are needed to achieve the business goal.
7. Use identified knowledge and skills to inform course objectives.
8. For each course objective, design and develop learning activities.

Notice that step 4 requires you to establish evaluation criteria before creating a curriculum. Although we will not (and cannot) know the results of TD initiatives until after they've been implemented, we can be more intentional about how we design, develop, and deliver initiatives so they're more likely to produce desired results. After all, in some cases, poorly implemented TD initiatives can be more damaging to organizations than if there had been no initiative at all, especially if they compromise business leaders' and employees' perceptions of the TD function or TD professionals.

In business process management, any business processes or procedures that don't yield results greater than the worth of their efforts are considered a waste. That's true with TD initiatives too. There is great danger in implementing TD initiatives that don't culminate in positive, intended change. Doing so can create the unfortunate impression among business leaders that talent development doesn't add value to their business and perhaps even detracts from it.

You must collaborate with business leaders to identify business challenges, which could be existing problems, such as declining revenues, or desirable opportunities, such as expanding the business into a new market. (Throughout the remainder of this book, business problems and opportunities are collectively referred to as "challenges.") Both parties need to agree that such a challenge is a priority for the business. You must understand the conditions of the challenge, including what caused a problem or what prompted an opportunity; the potential impact on the business; the possible implications of not addressing it; what its absence might lead to; and so forth.

This is an iterative and collaborative process between you and your business leaders that needs to result in a shared understanding of the challenge and an agreement about its causes. If such agreement is lacking, any subsequent TD initiatives would likely be futile because they would address the challenge from a single, incomplete perspective. Unfortunately, failed TD initiatives compromise the reputation and integrity of talent development, both the function and the people dedicated to it.

> Unfortunately, failed TD initiatives compromise the reputation and integrity of the talent development function and the people dedicated to it.

Because identifying business challenges is such a critical component, it's essential that you be skilled at it. We'll focus more on identifying business challenges and translating them into business goals in chapter 5. For now, though, let's assume that a business challenge has been identified, and there is a shared understanding of what it is and agreement around its causes. Once those conditions have been met, you must collaborate with business leaders to determine what needs to happen to address the challenge. You need to understand how people's thoughts, feelings, and actions (or behaviors) need to change to achieve desired results. To understand how the ways people think about, feel about, and do things are operationalized from a learning perspective, we'll explore a Think→Feel→Do Framework aligned with learning domains.

For example, a manufacturing company with the business challenge of increasing market share and revenue by introducing new products will likely train its sales force on product features, benefits, and proper use. It might also provide training or some form of self-guided, just-in-time learning content (such as job aids) for consumers on how to use the new products. Both are intended to result in people doing something new or differently. The more that people understand and appreciate product features and benefits—and the better they are at using the products—the more likely it is that the business will achieve its goals. This positions the company for increasing its market share and revenue.

Many practitioners in our field enter the discipline in unconventional ways, as I did. For those with business experience, the technical skills necessary to be successful in talent development might be brand-new. And for those with TD experience, the business skills necessary to be successful may be relatively new. Not convincing business leaders of the value that TD initiatives contribute toward achieving business goals can be one of the biggest, most insurmountable barriers to our success, and perhaps the success of the business. This book focuses on how you can win over business leaders' minds (how they *think*) and hearts (how they *feel*) by linking TD initiatives to evaluation criteria that define desired results.

Changing Behaviors

The work you do is all about designing initiatives that result in a behavior change, which ultimately results in improved performance outcomes that achieve desired business results. It's helpful to keep theories for behavior change top of mind because they not only inform your instructional design content but are also useful for changing the minds of your business leaders with respect to the value you add.

The Think→Feel→Do Framework

TD initiatives are based on the premise that how people currently *think* about, *feel* about, and *do* something is insufficient or ineffective for achieving a business goal. Such achievement requires changing behaviors. In both a current and future state, how someone *thinks* about something informs how they *feel* about it, and how they *feel* about it informs what they *do* in response. This Think→Feel→Do Framework (Figure 1-1) can help you understand how to change behaviors to achieve desired results.

Figure 1-1. The Think→Feel→Do Framework

When it comes to long-term, sustainable behavioral change, it's important that your initiatives address changing not just what people *do* but also how they *think* and *feel*. This is often done with one-on-one coaching. Consider the example in Figure 1-2.

Figure 1-2. Example of Think→Feel→Do

If we want to change our behaviors and actions toward our colleague, rather than preserving the initial thoughts and feelings that prompted us to avoid our colleague, we need to reframe them, as in Table 1-1.

Table 1-1. Reframing Behaviors

	Starting Posture	Reframed Posture
Think	My colleague is often abrupt and short with me, which leads me to believe they don't care for me or respect me.	My colleague is very busy working on projects for the team and doesn't have time to interact with me the way I would prefer.
Feel	I feel unimportant, unappreciated, and disrespected, which makes me uncomfortable and sad.	I feel grateful to my colleague for ensuring the success of our team, and I appreciate and admire their dedication and hard work.
Do	I avoid my colleague so I don't have negative experiences.	I offer to help my colleague.

In this example, simply changing the way you *think* about your colleague results in changing how you *feel* about that colleague, which in turn changes your behavior toward that colleague. Notice that while you focused on changing your own behavior rather than attempting to change your colleague's behavior, you might also experience a change in your colleague's behavior because of the change in your own behavior.

If we apply the Think→Feel→Do Framework to the thought offered earlier in this chapter that measurement and evaluation is likely the least preferred and performed TD activity, you can reframe your avoidance or fear of measurement and evaluation, as in Table 1-2.

Table 1-2. Reframing Measurement and Evaluation

	Starting Posture	Reframed Posture
Think	Measurement and evaluation is difficult, and I prefer to deal with people rather than data.	Measurement and evaluation is the best way to ensure that the work I do demonstrates to business leaders the value I add to achieving business results.
Feel	I worry that data might not demonstrate or prove that my work contributes in any meaningful way, so I would prefer to focus on the core work of designing, developing, and implementing TD initiatives.	I accept that data can help me understand what I need to do to improve the value I add.
Do	I avoid measuring anything more than learner reactions (Level 1) and learning that occurs during TD initiatives (Level 2).	I work diligently to design, develop, and implement TD initiatives that are created with the end in mind so that measurement and evaluation becomes much easier and tells a compelling story of the value added.

Simply focusing on changing peoples' actions without addressing the thoughts and feelings that produce those actions might result in unsustainable, temporary change. Consider weight-loss programs. People who make immediate changes to their actions (what, how, and when they eat) without any consideration to how they think or feel about food, nutrition, and health are unlikely to sustain any changes in their long-term behavior. This is one of the reasons many diets fail: They result in short-term behavior changes without addressing the dieter's underlying thoughts and feelings.

Telling people to change their behavior is insufficient for producing long-term behavioral change. In psychology, *behaviorism* is the theory that human and animal behaviors can be conditioned, or changed, without addressing thoughts or feelings. Behaviorism suggests that actions can be manipulated through rewards and punishments. For example, we might manipulate children to clean their bedroom through a promise of a reward or a threat of punishment, as shown in Table 1-3.

Table 1-3. Reward and Punishment

Action	Reward	Punishment
Clean bedroom	Receive allowance payment	Get grounded; cannot go outside and play with friends until the bedroom is cleaned

Notice that this example focuses only on changing observable actions, with no substantial or intentional change to how children think or feel. Rather than relying on rewards and punishments to condition actions, we might create more sustainable, long-term behavior change by appealing to the way children think and feel about cleaning their bedrooms (Table 1-4).

Table 1-4. Reframing Reward and Punishment

	Starting Posture	Reframed Posture
Think	Bedrooms are for sleeping, so cleanliness is unimportant.	Cleanliness is an important life skill. People associate cleanliness with organization and organization with success.
Feel	I don't mind having a messy room. I'd rather spend my time doing things more fun than cleaning.	I feel energized and compelled to clean. Being organized is satisfying.
Do	Do nothing and leave my room messy.	I'll clean my room and keep it tidy.

It might seem far-fetched that changing the way we think and feel about a given subject, idea, or experience can have a drastic impact on how we act. I have learned how powerful it is not because I conducted research or read scientific studies about it, but rather because I practice it every day in my own life to change my actions by reframing negative thoughts.

To illustrate this, I offer a personal example about a time I was expecting an overseas package to be delivered on a promised date. I waited with excitement and anticipation all day. After the expected delivery timeframe passed, I received a notification from the courier that they were unable to deliver the package that day. They informed me they were sending the package back to the delivery hub and would attempt delivery the following day. My first *thought* was that the courier had lied to me and was a terrible company. That thought resulted in me *feeling* disappointed, frustrated, and angry. Those feelings made me want to contact the courier, which would likely have wasted my time and theirs because it wasn't going to get the package delivered to me any sooner. Instead of placing that call, I decided to use my time and energy on reframing how I thought and felt about the situation. I had just spent a full day waiting for the package. The anticipation had brought me happiness and joy. Now that I had to wait yet another day for the package, I'd been given an opportunity to experience another day of anticipation and excitement. That new thought reframed my feelings. I felt relieved, happy, and excited. Those new feelings changed the way I acted—I didn't place an angry call to the courier. Just changing the way I thought and felt about the situation completely changed my mood and behavior. The lesson for me was that I cannot find happiness until I can find gratitude and joy in the pursuit of it. Otherwise, I'll always be chasing after something, which will prevent me from being present in and fully appreciating every moment.

The Three Learning Domains

We can align the Think→Feel→Do Framework with the three classic learning domains. All TD initiatives should address sustainably changing the way people think about (*cognitive* domain), feel about (*affective* domain), and do something (*psychomotor* domain) in the intentional pursuit of achieving a business goal. This, in turn, demonstrates the true value talent development brings to businesses and organizations.

For people's behaviors to change, existing behaviors need to be replaced with new ones. This is where you come in. Once you determine what new behaviors will enable the achievement of desired business results as part of needs assessment work, you can then design, develop, and implement initiatives that equip learners with the necessary knowledge, skills, and attitudes that correspond to the three primary learning domains:

- **Cognitive**—the way people think; what they know; knowledge
- **Affective**—the way people feel; attitudes
- **Psychomotor**—the way people do something; skills

Although these three learning domains were originally intended for traditional primary education, they've been co-opted by the TD profession, particularly as they relate to establishing course learning objectives for instructional design. (You can learn more about the three domains in Appendix A.) In the HR realm, these domains are often referred to as *knowledge* (cognitive domain), *skills* (psychomotor domain), and *attitudes* (affective domain), or KSAs (Table 1-5).

Table 1-5. Learning Domain Terminology

Framework	Learning Domain	Also Known As
Think	Cognitive	Knowledge
Feel	Affective	Attitudes
Do	Psychomotor	Skills

These learning domains provide a framework for writing course learning objectives, which is covered in chapter 7 as part of step 7 of the eight-step Evaluation-Focused Instructional Design Framework.

I remain optimistic that I can change the minds and hearts of my fellow TD professionals regarding measurement and evaluation, and I am dedicated to demonstrating how rethinking the role of measurement and evaluation can completely revolutionize how we approach adding value to the businesses we support. When we can join forces with business leaders and gain and build their commitment to attaining business results by defining and agreeing upon the metrics and measures to determine outputs and outcomes, we then have a framework to design and develop initiatives that deliver results.

Reimagining ADDIE

One way you can demonstrate your business acumen and your commitment to evaluation is to reimagine ADDIE, the framework inspired by a five-phase approach (analysis, design, development, implementation, and evaluation) to instructional design, developed by the United States Air Force (1993). That said, there is always room for adaptation, and the approach I use separates and disperses the *E* of ADDIE—evaluation—into three parts: E_C, which involves establishing evaluation criteria; E_I, which involves creating evaluation instruments; and E_E, which involves executing the evaluation of a training course. The reimagined ADDIE framework presented in this book includes the following phases:

- **A:** Analysis
- **E$_C$:** *Evaluation criteria*
- **D:** Design
- **E$_I$:** *Evaluation instruments*
- **D:** Develop
- **I:** Implement
- **E$_E$:** *Evaluation execution*

With this framework, you can use the evaluation criteria as an instructional design blueprint for designing, developing, and implementing meaningful learning programs.

Analysis

This first phase is an information-gathering inquiry phase, which you'll do in steps 1, 2, and 3 of the eight-step Evaluation-Focused Instructional Design Framework. You collaborate with business leaders to identify business challenges and determine how best to allocate people and resources to address those challenges. The analysis phase may involve several different analyses, including but not limited to business analysis and diagnostic analysis (root-cause and gap analyses), which are covered in more detail in chapter 5 and pertain directly to business results. Instructional designers should consider other analyses when analyzing training needs, such as a work-setting analysis, context analysis, and learner analysis.

Evaluation Criteria

During this phase, which you'll execute in step 4, you use the information collected and knowledge gained during the analysis phase to collaborate with business leaders on the measures, metrics, and targets that you intend to use to evaluate the success of a TD initiative. As part of the eight-step Evaluation-Focused Instructional Design Framework, evaluation criteria will be established for four levels of evaluation: reaction, learning, behavior or application, and results or impact. You'll use these criteria to determine training design content and to inform the design and development phases.

Design

Once you have completed the analysis phase and defined your evaluation criteria, you can propose the design for a TD initiative intended to address the business challenge identified in the analysis phase, which will happen in steps 5, 6, 7, and 8. The output of the design phase is a design outline that addresses the objectives of the initiative; what knowledge, skills, and attitudes will be addressed; what activities you will use to demonstrate proficiency; and what resources you will need. Many design outlines include a storyboard of what content will be presented, how it will be presented, when it will be presented, how long it will take, and so on. Generally, a business leader will review and approve an initiative's design before you develop it in the next phase.

During the design phase, you'll conduct a content analysis, which involves identifying the knowledge, skills, and attitudes that learners need to exhibit in the application environment (or work setting) to produce desired results. Then you'll use that information to establish course learning objectives that inform course learning activities.

Evaluation Instruments

During this phase, you will create all of the evaluation instruments. This can be done after the coursework is developed, but it's more beneficial to create the evaluation instruments first if the same individuals are creating the curriculum and evaluation instruments. Creating evaluation instruments first ensures that what will be measured is included in the course content. Learn more about creating evaluation instruments in Appendixes B and C.

Develop

Once an initiative's design and evaluation instruments have been reviewed and approved by a business leader, you can then build out the initiative during the development phase. This is when the initiative is actually created, including any collateral, materials, and media required to implement it. Generally, a business leader reviews and approves a development document before the initiative is implemented in the next phase.

Implement

This phase is the actual execution of the TD initiative—when you announce the TD initiative and learners are invited or required to attend. It's the phase when facilitation or instruction occurs—the "go live" or event portion of a TD initiative. This is the phase that is the most visible to the most people. What happens during implementation gets evaluated as part of the evaluation process because it relates to whether the TD initiative produced the desired results. The implementation phase could be very short or rather lengthy. For some TD initiatives, implementation might be a one-hour course. For others, it could be a yearlong leadership development program.

Evaluation Execution

This phase involves collecting and analyzing data to understand how an initiative changed learners' behaviors and whether it achieved the intended results. This book does not focus on the execution of evaluation, but if you follow the eight steps of the Evaluation-Focused Instructional Design Framework, you will be well positioned to evaluate your TD initiative.

Summary

It's important for TD professionals and business leaders alike to reframe talent development as business development. To accept that is to accept that people development is business development and businesses grow as people grow. Once you see your work that way, you can help your business leaders follow suit. One way to do that is to infuse measurement and evaluation into your work as a TD professional, especially when creating learning programs.

Partnering with business leaders is essential to your function's success. Demonstrating business acumen to business leaders by assisting with identifying and addressing business challenges can go a long way in changing how they think about, feel about, and behave toward talent development.

Reimagining the time-tested and prevalent ADDIE framework by placing an emphasis on evaluation and infusing it throughout the process can be an effective way to connect TD initiatives to business results. Approaching talent development as business development with the partnership of business leaders will not only change your experience as a TD professional, but it could also improve the engagement of your people and the success of your business.

Chapter 2
Connect to Your Stakeholders

Just as I did in my high-school teaching example in the introduction, you too must consider the various customers and stakeholders of the TD function. Knowing them is critical for aligning TD initiatives with business strategy, ensuring strong partnerships with business leaders, and adding value. To make a case and deliver results, this chapter focuses on identifying, prioritizing, and engaging those stakeholders.

Identify Your Customers and Other Stakeholders

For some organizations, the main customers of TD initiatives might be their employees. For others, it could be consumers who purchase initiatives from the organization for their own use. For still others, it might be third-party providers who purchase initiatives from the organization and provide them to their own customers. Some organizations may train customers who aren't employees or consumers but agents of the organization—for example, an organization might train volunteers to serve as volunteer leaders of other volunteers. Some organizations have a combination of the above.

If you accept the premise that all TD initiatives are intended to change behaviors (including actions) and culminate in desired results, start by asking, "Whose behaviors or actions are our initiatives intended to change?" and "What are the desired results?"

Be careful not to confuse beneficiaries with customers. Although they're sometimes the same, they are often quite different. For example, a hospital's TD function might provide staff training on how to interact with agitated patients. The training program might include how doctors and nurses can de-escalate and defuse situations and coach patients to reframe the thoughts that cause them to behave in agitated ways. In this case, the training course's consumers are doctors and nurses whose behaviors when dealing with agitated patients are changed. The beneficiaries are patients because the training benefits their interactions with the healthcare workers. Of course, ideally the behaviors of the agitated patients would also change (for example, they may retreat from a defensive posture and appear calmer) because of how their doctors and nurses interact with them, which is helpful for the beneficiaries and certainly appreciated by the healthcare workers.

Customers and beneficiaries are examples of *stakeholders*. The International Organization for Standardization defines a stakeholder as an "individual or group that has an interest in any decision or activity of an organization" (American Society for Quality n.d.). Another way to think about stakeholders is that they are individuals who are affected by the outcome of a project or initiative, or who have some level of interest in or control over it. Some might be significantly affected, while others might be only slightly affected.

To ensure that TD initiatives consider affected stakeholders when they're designed, developed, implemented, and evaluated, you must be able to identify the stakeholders and understand their various needs and motives. As part of your stakeholder analysis, you'll identify the reason each stakeholder "holds a stake" in your initiative—the *why*. For example, a sales executive holds a stake in the success of their company's sales results; therefore, they have a vested interest in the overall performance of a sales training course provided to salespeople. Because of their high degree of influence over and interest in company sales, and because they likely have the power of the purse—or the authority to authorize the use of resources (budget, technology, materials, or space)—they would be identified as a primary stakeholder who is deeply invested in the success of the initiative and who *must* be engaged significantly throughout the initiative.

There are multiple approaches to identifying and prioritizing stakeholders and their *whys*. Let's review three ways. Each can be done independently of the others or in combination. While the techniques might appear initially to compete with one another, I'll explain how I combine them after reviewing each approach.

Strategy 1: Primary, Secondary, and Tertiary Stakeholders

Your customers are only one group of the TD function's many stakeholders, and it's important to identify everyone. To differentiate between the degree to which stakeholders are affected—and to help prioritize the needs of the various stakeholder groups—one way to organize them is by grouping them into three categories:

- **Primary stakeholders**—individuals who are responsible and accountable for TD initiatives. For most initiatives, this includes the business leaders for whom the initiatives are created, as well as those who fund the initiatives. Other primary stakeholders include anyone responsible for implementing and managing the initiatives. Regulatory bodies and government agencies may be primary stakeholders.
- **Secondary stakeholders**—individuals who are affected by TD initiatives but are not responsible for their implementation or administration. For most initiatives, this includes those individuals whose behaviors should change because of the initiative: learners or participants. In addition, secondary stakeholders include beneficiaries, or those who are on the receiving end of learners' or participants' behavior changes (such as customers, patients, other colleagues, and members of the public). Shareholders might also be secondary stakeholders.
- **Tertiary stakeholders**—individuals who aren't immediately involved with TD initiatives but who may have some future interest. For example, an employee who may eventually go through the initiative at some point in their career would be a tertiary stakeholder with some level of interest in the initiative (Russ-Eft and Preskill 2009).

Identifying stakeholders can be complicated, but it's a necessary activity if you want to ensure that the initiatives you design and deliver are capable of producing desired results. Without understanding who has a vested interested in the initiatives—and what those interests are—you run the risk of satisfying the needs of one stakeholder group while completely disregarding the needs of another. For example, if you focus only on making sure a training program is fun for learners, they may absolutely enjoy participating, but if the program doesn't result in learners going back to their jobs and changing their behaviors in meaningful ways to produce desired results, then business leaders' needs will not have been met.

Without understanding who has a vested interested in the initiatives—and what those interests are—you run the risk of satisfying the needs of one stakeholder group while completely disregarding the needs of another.

Strategy 2: Sphere of Control

Another way to organize stakeholders is something I call the "sphere of control" (Figure 2-1). I find this tool particularly helpful in teasing out the various stakeholders for any initiative that is intended to result in behavior change.

Figure 2-1. Sphere of Control

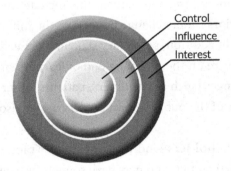

Using this approach, you group stakeholders into three categories:
- **Control**—people who can make intentional decisions about and have full control of changing their own behaviors. While talent development initiatives (and facilitators and instructors) can only attempt to influence changes in learners' behaviors, learners can control their own behaviors. Anyone who has ever dealt with other human beings knows that the only person who can control behavior

is the person exhibiting or performing the behavior. In the example about doctors and nurses undergoing training for interacting with agitated patients, the training program is intended to result in doctors and nurses controlling their own behaviors (by responding neutrally, not matching the patient's tone and tenor, helping reframe the patient's thoughts and feelings that may be causing the unruly behavior, and addressing conditions that enhance the patient's comfort). The training, however, is *not* intended to control the behaviors of agitated patients. Rather, training is intended to *influence* their behaviors by controlling a change in doctors' and nurses' behaviors. There is often confusion around controlling other people's behaviors. Some people mistakenly believe that behaviorism—the use of rewards and punishments to affect behavior—is a form of control, but this is really only a tactic for influencing behaviors, not controlling them.

- **Influence**—people whose behaviors an initiative is intended to influence (with a complete understanding that they can't be controlled). In the same example, patients are the stakeholders of influence because the training for doctors and nurses can influence behavior changes in the patients.

- **Interest**—people whose behaviors you have a vested interest in but who you might not have any control or influence over. For example, you don't have control or influence over the behaviors of an agitated patient's family and friends. To the extent that families' and friends' behaviors influence the behaviors of patients, doctors and nurses have an interest in their behavior. For example, my cousin is a hospice nurse, and her work with dying patients occasionally is influenced by the thoughts, feelings, and behaviors of relatives. She noted that, from a cultural perspective, food is an expression of love among some groups, and even though it might be in the patient's best interest to stop eating at a certain point in the day or to refrain from certain foods, relatives might continue to attempt to feed them out of love. Although my cousin tries to influence the family's behavior by expressing why certain foods aren't helpful, sometimes relatives reject her advice. Regardless, she has a vested interest in their behaviors.

When using the sphere of control for determining stakeholders, consider the following:

- **Whose behaviors are the TD initiative intended to *directly* change?** More specifically, which people will acquire new (or improve existing) knowledge, skills, or attitudes as a result of participating in the initiative? These are the individuals who would be identified as stakeholders in the "control" circle.

- **Whose behaviors are the initiative intended to *indirectly* change?** More specifically, which people will *experience* the changed behaviors of those who participated in the initiative? These are the individuals who would be identified as stakeholders in the "influence" circle.

- **Who requested that the TD initiative be offered?** Who ultimately benefits from the changed behaviors of those in the control and influence circles? These are the individuals who would be identified as stakeholders in the "interest" circle.

One of the things I like about this approach is that it places the focus on those whose behaviors will be changed by participating in initiatives rather than on those who sponsor and fund them. To the extent you can successfully demonstrate how prioritizing the needs of the stakeholders in the "control" circle will ultimately lead to achieving a business goal, the business's needs will be prioritized over primary stakeholders' individual motives.

To the extent you can successfully demonstrate how prioritizing the needs of the stakeholders in the "control" circle will ultimately lead to achieving a business goal, the business's needs will be prioritized over primary stakeholders' individual motives.

Strategy 3: Level of Influence and Interest

Another way to organize various stakeholders is to categorize them by their level of influence and interest, as shown in the quadrants of the matrix in Figure 2-2, also known as a power map, which you'll use in chapter 3 to make a business case for talent development.

Figure 2-2. Stakeholder Analysis Power Map

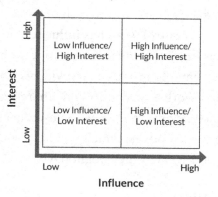

Consider each identified stakeholder and determine their degree of influence (low to high) and degree of interest (low to high). Then place them on a grid with influence as the X-axis and interest as the Y-axis. This provides a visual representation of where stakeholders fall, which can be useful in prioritizing stakeholders to ensure they're appropriately targeted for the right approach to engagement. A benefit of using this approach is that some stakeholders may wield high influence but lack interest in the initiative. The power map could help you identify them and prioritize your efforts to boost their interest by helping them understand how the initiative will benefit the business.

> A benefit of using this approach is that some stakeholders may wield high influence but lack interest in the initiative. The power map could help you identify them and prioritize your efforts to boost their interest by helping them understand how the initiative will benefit the business.

The Strategies in Action

These three approaches are not inherently correlated with one another, nor are they mutually exclusive. Individuals identified as primary stakeholders aren't necessarily the same as those identified in the "control" circle, and individuals identified in the "control" circle aren't necessarily those who have high influence and high interest. In fact, you can use these frameworks in combination with one another. For example, once you identify primary, secondary, and tertiary stakeholders, within each of those three categories, you can determine who has control, who has influence, and who has interest. The three approaches simply provide a framework for how to organize and prioritize various stakeholder groups or individuals. Whichever approach you use, the important work is to identify and differentiate each stakeholder group. This way you'll be able to engage them in meaningful, productive ways and prioritize their motives, which will help you work through any competing motives and agendas they might have.

Engage Stakeholders

Once you identify and prioritize your stakeholders, the next step is to strategize how best to involve them. If you identified a person or group, you should engage them in some meaningful way to harness or strategically manage their existing influence and interest. Engagement can take the form of simply communicating information to them, soliciting information from them, consulting them on decisions, seeking their approval, or requesting allocation of resources (such as time, people, money, or materials). Stakeholder engagement includes strategizing how to involve each identified person to ensure the success of your TD initiative.

One of the most important reasons for categorizing and prioritizing stakeholders is to differentiate the extent to which you must engage each one throughout the initiative, including when, what, and how to communicate with them; when to seek their input; and when to secure their approval. How and when stakeholders are involved can have a tremendous impact on their:

- Level of support and buy-in
- Allocation of resources
- Commitment to the initiative's success
- Attention to the initiative when there are competing priorities

Stakeholder engagement can make or break a TD initiative. By meaningfully engaging stakeholders, you build commitment to the initiative and its success by fostering trust, confidence, and support. If you fail to gain—or even worse, lose—the trust, confidence, or support of stakeholders for the initiative, it puts the initiative at risk of failure, and it could be very damaging to the reputation of the TD function and its ability to partner with the business to add real value.

Label Stakeholders as Resisters, Compliers, or Adopters

Stakeholders, regardless of whether they are primary, secondary, or tertiary—and regardless of their degree of control, interest, or influence—will demonstrate behaviors relative to the initiative. For each stakeholder you've identified, you can decide which of the following three categories they fall into:

- **Resisters** are stakeholders who are opposed to the initiative. Their reasons for resistance may range from fear to a genuinely held conviction that the initiative isn't in the best interest of the business, its employees, or its customers. Resisters can be active or passive. Active resisters tend to compromise the image and reputation of the initiative to get others to view it in a negative light. In my experience, those who resist change often do so because they don't sufficiently understand the need for the program, they perceive the program to be more effort than it is worth, or they have something to lose (such as power) because of it. For example, I once worked with a business leader who was the go-to expert on a database the organization relied on to conduct business. When the organization decided to pursue an alternative technology solution, that business leader resisted from the beginning. They were the clear authority over the existing database, and their status was threatened by a new solution because it meant they were no longer the perceived expert. That resulted in them feeling not only a sense of loss and mourning for the old database, but also a sense of resentment for any replacement solution.

- **Compliers** are stakeholders who neither openly support nor reject an initiative but are willing to passively accept it out of fear, self-preservation, or apathy. They're essentially willing to *comply* with the initiative. Compliers will go along with what they perceive they must, but they can't be expected to demonstrate commitment and advocacy in encouraging or convincing others to support the initiative. For example, while working with employees on plans to return to the office after working from home for two and a half years during the

COVID-19 pandemic, I encountered many compliers. They were willing to go back because they had to keep their jobs, but they didn't agree with it, they didn't want to do it, and they certainly weren't encouraging others to see the benefits of doing so.

- **Adopters** are stakeholders who wholeheartedly understand and appreciate the value of the initiative and commit to it and its success. In many ways, these stakeholders serve as evangelists who help convince other stakeholders of the initiative's importance. Failing to appropriately engage adopters may alienate them. These stakeholders generally need to be involved to maintain their support. For example, when I've presented on the topic of this book to fellow TD professionals, I've witnessed many of them become adopters. They took my framework for designing meaningful initiatives with evaluation in mind back to their own organizations and have evangelized the process. Many of them asked me to speak to their teams, and they supported me writing this book. They are adopters! I do my best to keep them actively engaged so they'll continue to position the TD functions in their organizations for success. Their success is our profession's success, and our profession's success is essential for creating a world that works better.

Stakeholders' positions and motives may be dynamic rather than static—they can evolve over time, depending on how you engage them. You should also recognize, for instance, that not all your primary stakeholders will be adopters, nor will all your tertiary stakeholders be resisters. Within each stakeholder category, you'll likely have varying levels of commitment. And a stakeholder who is an adopter could become a resister if their interests are disregarded. So, you will want to continue to take the pulse of your stakeholders to monitor for changes in interest, influence, and advocacy.

Move Your Stakeholders Along the Adoption Continuum

Knowing that there are resisters (in addition to compliers and adopters) raises the question of which stakeholder category is worth investing the most time and effort in throughout an initiative to move them to a higher category (or prevent them from sliding into a lower category). I faced this dilemma as a teacher, too. I had to decide which group of students I should spend more time with. Using the traditional grading structure, I could focus on working with:

- **A students**, who had already demonstrated proficiency, to reinforce their learning and help them maintain their success
- **B students**, who might become A students with a little more work
- **C students**, who weren't failing but also not quite succeeding; they had potential to become B or D students
- **D and F students**, who were underperforming

Ultimately I didn't want to lose the support of the adopters (A and B students) or waste the potential of the compliers (C students), so I made time to engage them. For each individual resister (D and F students), I had to determine how much time and effort it would take to move them along the adoption continuum to at least become compliers. If I deemed it worth the effort, I did what I could. For those resisters who weren't at all willing to do their part to learn and be successful, I had to accept that they simply couldn't be influenced no matter what I tried.

With respect to your TD initiatives, you should also consider how to move your stakeholders along the continuum (Figure 2-3).

Figure 2-3. Adoption Continuum

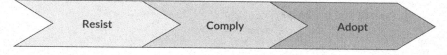

Additionally, it's important to manage the expectations and needs of these various stakeholders. Knowing where a stakeholder falls in the continuum is critical to managing their expectations. In chapter 6, I explore an approach for managing the expectations of business leaders (as stakeholders), particularly as it relates to results that TD initiatives can deliver.

Prioritize Stakeholders' Needs

Once you've identified your stakeholders and you understand their views on a TD initiative, it's important to prioritize them, their needs, and their motives. Assuming every stakeholder and their needs and motives are equally important is to mistakenly assume that no stakeholders matter more than others. While it may feel awkward, prioritizing certain stakeholders ensures the success of your initiative.

When prioritizing the many stakeholders in my teaching example, I determined that students and their needs and motives were among the most important for me as a teacher, because if I wasn't successful with them, there was no way I would be successful with anyone else. That said, I certainly didn't discount all the other stakeholders. I simply accepted that I had to prioritize my students. Further, students' needs and motives were certainly different from those of the other stakeholder groups, so prioritizing them didn't mean completely rejecting the needs and motives of the other stakeholders.

One approach to prioritizing stakeholders to ensure their engagement in the initiative is to categorize them into three groups:

- **Must**—stakeholders whom you absolutely must engage. How and how often you engage these stakeholders may vary.
- **Should**—stakeholders whom you should engage because of their degree of interest and influence, but they are not as high of a priority as those in the "must" category.
- **Could**—stakeholders whom you could engage, but if you have limited time and resources, the implication of not engaging them as much as those in the "must" and "should" categories is less significant to the success of the initiative.

The Engagement Process

No matter how you categorize or prioritize stakeholders, how you engage each category—or even the individuals within each category—may vary. For a stakeholder to become an adopter, a resister, or a complier, they need to be sufficiently *aware* of what the initiative is, what it entails, and what it's intended to do before they decide whether they support it, despise it, or are apathetic to it. Building this sense of awareness for all stakeholders through intentional engagement is important, and the way you approach their engagement can have a tremendous impact on which category a stakeholder ultimately falls into.

One of the most important ways to engage stakeholders is to help them understand how the initiative will improve the business, and in doing so, help them understand the *WIIFM (What's in it for me?)*. Without investing this effort into all stakeholders, you miss an opportunity to move resisters to compliers and compliers to adopters.

You'll want to determine which person or people will be responsible for engaging each stakeholder (the *who*), the way in which stakeholders will be engaged (the *how*), and the timing and frequency for engaging stakeholders (the *when*). For example, if you're working on an initiative for a sales training program that's intended to help your company achieve a sales revenue goal, you would likely identify the sales executive as a primary stakeholder. From there, you need to determine the who, how, and when of the engagement process:

- **Who**—the person responsible for engaging the sales executive might be the initiative's lead or the TD executive. It's someone clearly identified on the TD team who is empowered to collaborate and negotiate with the sales executive on the initiative. This person will generally have decision-making authority to ensure that decisions are made in the best interest of the company and with desired results in mind.
- **How**—the way in which the "who" will ultimately engage the stakeholder. How will they be intentional about listening to stakeholders and soliciting their input? Will they meet with them in person? Will the stakeholders' blessing or explicit permission be solicited? Will stakeholders only be consulted? Will they be updated on the status and progress of the initiative? Will they be invited to participate in meetings? Will they be needed to participate in the design and development of the initiative? Will they be copied on correspondence related to the initiative? Will they be invited to provide guidance and feedback? The considerations are many.
- **When**—the timeline and cadence for engaging the stakeholders. Will stakeholders be involved on a regular or ad hoc basis? When will you meet with them? When will their input be solicited? When will their approval be sought?

Stakeholder identification, prioritization, and engagement are vital to the success of all TD initiatives. Once we understand who our customers are, or whom we exist to provide learning for, we can work toward aligning the TD function to business strategy.

Summary

Everything you do as a TD professional involves, influences, or affects others—sometimes directly and immediately, and sometimes peripherally and in some distant future. Therefore, nothing you do in talent development should be done independent of your stakeholders. Investing the time and effort in identifying, understanding, prioritizing, and engaging your stakeholders can make or break the success of your TD initiatives.

You approach all TD initiatives with a motive: to improve business results by changing behaviors. To understand what desired results the business wishes to achieve, and which learner behaviors need to be changed to achieve them, you need to seek out and understand your stakeholders' motives. Where motives differ, you must find common ground to determine the business results and learner behavior changes that satisfy the most important stakeholders.

Chapter 3
Position Your TD Function to Produce Results

Unfortunately, there is no one-size-fits-all approach to getting your business leaders' buy-in for your initiatives. It depends on myriad factors, including your business leaders' past experiences with TD professionals and how those business leaders perceive the TD function's role within the organization. It's imperative to invest time in ensuring your TD function is organized in a way that makes business sense and maximizes value the your organization. After clearly identifying your customers—those who consume and are affected by your initiatives—you're prepared to rethink how your function can best support the organization, as well as present a case to your business leaders for enacting any changes within your function.

For meaningful, sustainable change to occur, it is vital that the TD function be appropriately organized and staffed. While it may seem like a logical place to start—to reimagine the TD function before introducing new ways of engaging business leaders (and other stakeholders) through TD initiatives that are aligned to business strategy—it may make sense in your organization to first implement one or more TD initiatives following the eight-step Evaluation-Focused Instructional Design Framework to demonstrate to business leaders just what impact and value talent development is capable of adding and using those wins to elevate the importance of talent development for your business.

Examine Your Company's Principles

Convincing business leaders of the TD function's importance may run the gamut from extremely difficult to relatively easy, depending on the organization's philosophy of talent—*its people*—and its mission, vision, and values. Understanding the importance and role of each factor is essential to customizing a business case for a renewed TD function that benefits your organization.

What Makes Your Business Successful?

To make a case for how your TD initiatives can contribute to the success of your business, you'll have to demonstrate a comprehensive understanding of the business. Undoubtedly, successful organizations place tremendous value on several factors necessary for their viability, sustainability, and success, but let's consider seven primary factors. To better learn the business, invest time and effort into understanding each of the following:

- **Strategy**—how the business achieves its goals and objectives. For example, a business may have a high price point targeted to a wealthy segment of a consumer population, or it may have a low price point to sell high volumes to lower-income consumers.
- **Products and services**—what *need* the business offers and satisfies for its consumers. Consumers may be drawn to a particular business and exhibit loyalty because of the products or services the company offers. For example, as an avid aquarist, I trust certain companies to have high-quality products that will maintain the health and viability of my aquariums. I trust one company for fish food, another for aquarium filters, another for aquarium heaters, and another for marine salt mix. When I'm in the market for any of those goods, I patronize those businesses because of the quality and durability of the products they produce, irrespective of their business strategy or who works for them.
- **People**—the talent that comprises the business. For example, a restaurant may employ chefs who are renowned for their cuisine and consistently deliver high-quality gourmet food. When you patronize a business because of its people, that talent becomes their

competitive advantage. Another common industry for consumer loyalty to people is cosmetology; you might go to your hairdresser because you want the particular quality and technique they offer. You may not have a loyalty to the business, but you might have a loyalty to a person (or people) who works for the business. If they move to another company, you might follow them because you trust them and admire their talent. In my experience, business leaders are more likely to invest in people and retain them when they are the business's primary competitive advantage. If those businesses can keep those people, they can also keep their loyal customers. Hence, these businesses may be more inclined to place a high importance on talent development and view TD initiatives as investments rather than expenses.

- **Facilities and real estate**—the physical footprint of the business; where it exists in proximity to its consumers. For example, a business may open in a high-traffic tourist area to sell souvenirs at a premium, or a pharmacy may determine that it's wise to open on neighborhood corners to attract traffic from multiple directions.

- **Equipment**—the tools the business uses to produce its goods and services. For example, the taste of a pizzeria's pizza may be affected by a pizza oven—whether it's electric, gas, coal, or wood-fired—and how high the temperature gets. It's very difficult for consumers to replicate the taste and texture of pizza made in restaurants because home ovens don't heat to the temperature required to produce a rapid bake with leopard spotting, which is the light charring of the dough that creates a crispy outer and pillowy inner crust.

- **Brand**—the perceived value of the business's products or services. For example, a consumer may acquire a degree of prestige by being seen consuming, wearing, or using items from a high-end merchandiser. Therefore, consumers may covet the brand. To preserve the brand, a business may take strict measures to protect its intellectual property. When I worked for Harry & David, known for its holiday fruitcake, the company had to ensure others couldn't duplicate the recipe, which would diminish the brand. This was so important to the company that no one person knew the entire recipe. Rather, the recipe was separated into parts, and each part was secured in a safe. Only one person was permitted to work on each part of the recipe, and they would never be granted access to the other part. In addition, the company required employees to sign nondisclosure and noncompete agreements to protect the intellectual property and preserve the brand.

- **Markets and market share**—a business may attempt to dominate a market by having a significant market share that edges out the competition. For example, a business might thrive because a community (the market) has a predilection for the particular brand of snack or beverage the business produces.

One way to understand the importance and role of these factors in your organization is to talk with your business executives about them. Another is to review your organization's budget to determine how money is spent relative to each factor. Draw on your understanding of your organization's annual expense budget (how it spends its revenue) and its mission, vision, and values (how it expresses its brand), as well as on your own experience with the organization.

If you were to choose one of the seven preceding factors as the biggest driver of competitive advantage for your organization, which would rise to the top? How would you rank the seven in order of importance? Although it may seem like a challenging exercise, if you assume they are all equally important, you are essentially accepting that none of them independently stands as your competitive advantage. In other words, when everything is the most important, nothing is the most important. Complete the "Rank Your Competitive Advantage" activity on the next page to consider your business further.

How you ranked these factors as they exist in your organization might be exactly how you would prioritize them. To the extent there are discrepancies, however, opportunities exist to make a case for how talent development initiatives might help shift prioritization.

Rank Your Competitive Advantage

Considering your organization today, and drawing on how the organization spends money, how would you rank the following factors from 1 to 7, with one representing the most significant?

Current State

Rank (1–7)	Factor
	Strategy
	Products and Services
	People
	Facilities and Real Estate
	Equiment
	Brand
	Markets and Market Share

If you could unilaterally rank these factors to maximize the culture, success, viability, and relevance of your organization, how would you rank them? Remember, how these items are ranked generally informs your organization's budget.

Ideal Future State

Rank (1–7)	Factor
	Strategy
	Products and Services
	People
	Facilities and Real Estate
	Equipment
	Brand
	Markets and Market Share

Identify How Your Business Perceives the Role of People

Understanding the importance and role of each factor helps you understand the role of people relative to your business. Knowing how your business perceives the importance of people is helpful in understanding how it perceives talent development: a necessary business investment or a discretionary cost.

You might typically equate talent development professionals with instructional designers, facilitators, evaluators, and the like. A lot of successful TD professionals wear many hats beyond these core competencies, including adopting—and adapting—the work of sociologists, market researchers, investigators, and reporters. To be successful, you need to examine corporate cultures as a sociologist would study a society. You need to act like a market researcher to understand the needs and wants of businesses and people. You need to act like a detective who exhibits the right amount of curiosity to solve mysteries or explain why events occur. You need to act like a reporter to tell the stories of why talent development is critical and how it affects a business.

To determine your organization's people philosophy, step outside your traditional TD role and your organization, and imagine you're a sociologist discovering a new culture. For this exercise, *culture* is the social order of an organization, shaped by the behaviors, values, and beliefs held by those within it. It's informed by behaviors that are rewarded and punished. It's influenced by power dynamics and how decisions get made in the organization. It's primarily apparent in how people engage with one another, how they are expected to behave toward one another, and how they are expected to perform. The corporate culture reveals a lot about the role of people and how they are valued in an organization.

The value of people can range from employees being seen as a necessary but easily replaced resource to employees being seen as a competitive advantage (what sets an organization apart from others). In fact, at Rotary International, we rebranded our HR function as "Global People and Talent" and elevated the top HR role to the organization's executive management team to convey the importance of people within our organization. We don't view humans as resources; we view our employees as people who apply their talent to resources to generate value for the organization. We were intentional about using both the words *people* and *talent*, even though people possess talent:

- **People**—we chose *people* to express that we care about our employees 24 hours a day, seven days a week—not just when they're performing their jobs. Furthermore, we ensure that our employees have appropriate work-life integration, which includes the flexibility to work when and how it makes the most sense. Our employment benefits are designed to give our employees peace of mind that they'll have comfort and security during their employment and in retirement, they won't be bankrupted by medical emergencies, and they will have paid time away from work to ensure their health and well-being and to do the things they love with the people they love. Without our people, we couldn't succeed.

- **Talent**—we chose *talent* to express our desire to grow and develop our people to be successful in their current roles and for future roles that would be mutually beneficial to their career growth and our success as an organization. Our Global Talent and Organization Development team makes sure this is a priority for us.

Aspirational Versus Actualized Culture

As you explore the role of people in your business, you might discover a difference between *aspirational culture* (idealized culture), and how the culture exists in reality—the *actualized culture*. Incidentally, aspirational cultures are usually easier to initially identify because they're how organizations' cultures and brands are expressed. Mission statements, vision statements, values, brand propositions, and the like are expressions of how organizations see themselves and how they desire others to see them. But sometimes there is a real disconnect between an aspirational culture and an actualized culture. For example, an organization may say it cares about diversity, equity, and inclusion, but its employees from marginalized groups may report otherwise. This creates a conflict between the aspirational culture and the actualized culture. Because aspirational cultures are what tend to be documented, an outsider would likely be able to identify the aspirational culture but would need to investigate to learn how employees within that culture perceive it.

While there is nothing wrong with aspirational cultures and values, they should exist only if they serve as a road map for how an organization is going to achieve them. Absent that commitment to actualizing an aspirational culture, an aspirational culture is meaningless. People are generally more concerned about what cultures and values actually are, rather than what they could be. Imagine that a culture claims to value freedom and equality, but its people experience oppression and hierarchy. Such aspirational cultures and values risk being perceived as hypocritical.

If an organization has an aspirational culture and values, the organization should also be reflective and honest about what its actualized culture and values are. This acknowledgment creates transparency and serves as a reminder of the work that needs to be done to shift the culture from aspirational to actualized. So, as an example, an organization wishing to actualize aspirational values might communicate them to its people by using a table similar to Table 3-1.

Table 3-1. Actualizing Aspirational Values

Current State (Actualized Value)	Future State (Aspirational Value)	Strategy	Result
Control: Decisions are controlled by top leaders.	**Empowerment:** Our people are trusted to make decisions.	• Leaders will be trained on delegation and evaluated accordingly. • Employees will be trained on decision making and consulted about which decisions to make to do their job.	The right decisions are made by the right people at the right level.
Exclusion: Only long-tenured employees who are perceived to have power are listened to.	**Inclusion:** Our employees' voices matter and are regularly solicited and considered.	• Leaders will be held accountable for fostering greater inclusion. • Employees will be regularly surveyed to ensure they feel included.	The right people are "at the table" and included in the right discussions necessary for better engagement and decision making.

Early in my career, I served as the leader of a talent and organization development function for an organization that had hired a new CEO, who was brought in to reimagine how work was organized and performed (and in some cases, by whom). I was tapped as a facilitator to lead several workshops with the executive management team, which included an executive retreat to articulate what they wanted the corporate culture to be: the aspirational culture. As part of the retreat, the executive team identified several corporate values they thought were imperative for all employees to embody for the success of the organization. Among the several values they selected was "professional development."

While I was glad the executive team understood the importance of talent development, I had two immediate reactions:

- **I wished they had not labeled the value "professional development."** In my experience, employees interpret that to be event-based learning, where they attend a course for which the organization paid. Professional development was perceived as external learning opportunities that required funding. To avoid this interpretation, I would have preferred *continuous learning* or another descriptor connoting that learning happens every day and everywhere, not just in a classroom but also at employees' desks, in conference rooms, around the watercooler, and so on. Also, learning isn't didactic; it doesn't occur only when a facilitator teaches a participant new knowledge or skills. Instead, every employee is both a teacher and a learner. Nevertheless, the fact that leadership placed significant importance on the organization's people by way of this value was a huge step in the right direction.

- **I understood very clearly that "professional development" was aspirational, not actualized.** For employees to accept the value as real and not idealized, clearly more work had to be done. Sure, there already existed opportunities for employees to learn and grow, and the executive management team was accounting for these programs (such as new-hire orientation, soft-skills training courses, hard-skills training courses, and tuition reimbursement). However, as noted before, I knew employees considered professional development to be funding to attend conferences, take certificate programs offered by training vendors, and participate in external courses. Naming the value *professional development* presented a challenge about how to reframe it in a way that didn't just mean company-provided funding for employees to attend a training course or conference. Given that this value didn't come with any additional funding, I was very concerned that employees wouldn't agree that the organization truly valued professional development.

Not only did we need to demonstrate that professional development was already partially actualized, if it was going to be an aspirational value, the organization would need to demonstrate its commitment to making sure it was fully actualized. Otherwise, employees would reject that this was an organizational value. I approached the executive team with a proposal acknowledging that we had opportunities to be serious about actualizing the value. I proposed introducing a new professional-development-hours program at the same time that we unveiled the new set of values to our employees. This program would provide a minimum of 40 hours a year for every employee to use however they wanted, so long as the time was invested in their professional growth and development and the time and activities were preapproved by their manager as part of a professional development plan. The program didn't include any funding whatsoever (other than the sunk labor costs because the organization would pay employees for their time anyway).

While the proposal was initially received favorably, and the executives liked the idea of rolling out a new professional development program to demonstrate its importance, some expressed concern about the amount of time employees would be able to spend on their professional development—time that business leaders viewed as unproductive insofar as work not being performed. Some executives, including the CFO, believed it was simply too much nonwork time. He countered that we start with eight hours, or one business day, a year. I was prepared with a response that I hoped would change the way he thought and felt about it. I offered this set of facts:

- The organization occupies several floors of a downtown high-rise office building.
- Each day, all 575 headquarters employees had to use either stairs or elevators to traverse the building.
- On average, each employee spent 15 minutes a day either waiting for or riding an elevator.
- There are 365 days in nonleap years. Removing weekends, that leaves approximately 260 weekdays. Reduce that by 10 to account for annual holidays; take another 10 for sick days, off-site work assignments, and so forth, and another 20 for vacation time. That leaves about 220 workdays in the building. (This was in prepandemic 2020, when most of our employees worked every day in the office.)

- Fifteen minutes a day waiting for and riding elevators over 220 days amounts to 3,300 minutes, or 55 hours. That's 55 hours per employee per year doing nothing but waiting for and riding elevators!
- If we're OK with our employees spending more time on elevators than investing in their professional development, then we really need to reconsider professional development as a value.

Without any further discussion, the CFO was convinced, and the CEO ended the discussion by approving the 40-hour professional development program. That program still exists and was key to actualizing an aspirational value. By using the elevator data I collected, I reframed the conversation and helped the executive team understand the importance of investing in professional development, especially if we claim that it is an important corporate value.

All too often, what businesses claim to value is not always what employees experience. Another area of talent development where I see this happen frequently is succession planning. Many businesses purport to take succession planning seriously, yet they continue to hire key (that is, critical or leadership-level) positions externally. If you want to know if succession planning is aspirational or actualized, all you need to do is analyze how many internal candidates were promoted into key or leadership roles, and how many are qualified to apply for those positions.

Consider your organization's culture. Differentiate between the elements that are aspirational versus actualized. Think about how you can help close the gap and actualize aspirational elements. This is one of the many ways that you can add value to the business you support.

Articulate Your Mission, Vision, and Values

As you consider the role of people in your organization by examining your corporate culture, you'll want to review your business's mission, vision, and values—whether they're aspirational or actualized. Mission statements, vision statements, and values are considered artifacts of culture, which are those elements of culture created by people that can be seen or felt and convey a sense of meaning about the culture to others. Just as your organization should have these common cultural artifacts, well-organized and well-managed TD functions should have clearly defined missions, visions, and values that align with those of their organization. These statements can be useful in building rapport with business leaders. They need to understand why the TD function exists, what you do, how you work with the business, and what value you add. Clearly articulated missions, visions, and values can be very useful in conveying to business leaders how well you understand the business and the role you can play in enabling and supporting its success.

Established TD functions may have an existing mission statement, vision statement, and set of values that you may want to revisit and refresh. New or proposed functions will need to articulate their mission, vision, and values.

Mission

A mission is a brief description of what a business does and why it exists. It's an expression of the brand and the value provided to those served. Another way to think about a mission statement is that it's the *what*.

For example, the mission of the Global People and Talent business unit within Rotary International is "Our passion is people: Helping employees gives us our greatest satisfaction. That is why we support, empower, and develop them to their fullest potential so that they may make positive and lasting contributions to Rotary and its Secretariat." Everything we do as a function is aligned with our mission:

- **What we do:** Support, empower, and develop people
- **Why we do it:** So that they may make positive and lasting contributions to Rotary and its Secretariat
- **Whom we do it for:** Rotary's employees (directly), Rotary's members and participants (indirectly), and Rotary's beneficiaries (indirectly)

Your TD mission statement should be very brief—a sentence or a very short paragraph. The most meaningful mission statements are easily remembered. Often referred to as "elevator speeches" because they're short enough to share on an elevator ride, mission statements should be memorable for those who recite them and those who hear them. And more important, mission statements should be simple enough to always be top of mind so TD professionals can readily determine if their work aligns with and contributes to their organization's mission.

What's Your Mission?

1. Consider these questions when formulating a mission statement:
   - What problem do we solve?
   - What is our purpose?
   - Whom do we exist to serve?
   - What products or services do we offer to accommodate a demand?
   - What sets us apart from everyone else? What do we do that is unique?
2. Take a look at these examples:
   - ATD: "Empower professionals to develop talent in the workplace"
   - Feeding America: "To advance change in America by ensuring equitable access to nutritious food for all in partnership with food banks, policymakers, supporters, and the communities we serve"
   - IACET: "To accredit providers of high-quality learning and promote continuous improvement"
3. Write your own mission statement or revise an existing one.

Vision

A vision is a brief description of why you do what you do. It's an aspirational, desired impact. Effective vision statements are succinct expressions intended to motivate and inspire behaviors that result in a desired impact. Whereas a mission statement captures what you do, a vision statement captures why you do it—the sought-after future state.

The vision of the Global People and Talent function of Rotary International is "A workplace where everyone has an extraordinary employee experience." Why do we support, empower, and develop our people (*the what*)? Because we want everyone who works at Rotary to have an extraordinary employee experience (*the why*). That doesn't mean we expect every employee to always be pleased about everything, but even on their worst day, we want them to have a strong affinity for Rotary as their employer. We want to build strong psychological contracts with them so that it becomes more difficult for them to leave than to stay—and not just because of salary and benefits, but because the way Rotary shows up for employees during moments that matter (such as new-hire orientation, medical leave, promotions, or significant personal challenges) strengthens the bond between them. Aligning our TD work to our mission (*the what*) helps us achieve our vision (*the why*)—to ensure our employees realize an extraordinary employee experience.

A particularly useful technique in helping you articulate your TD function's vision is the "five whys" technique (also known as "5Y"), which we briefly discussed in the introduction of this book. Introduced as a quality assurance tool in the 1930s by Sakichi Toyoda, a Japanese industrialist and the founder of Toyota (Ohno 1988), the "five whys" has been co-opted by organization development practitioners to identify root causes of problems rather than simply focusing on their symptoms. It's as simple as it sounds: Given a problem, ask yourself, "Why?" and go at least five layers deep—or until you get to a root cause rather than a symptom.

To formulate a vision statement with 5Y, use your mission statement and ask, "Why?" five times. For example, if the mission is "To prioritize meaningful, high-value TD initiatives that contribute to the success of Acme Inc.," you would ask, "Why?" five times to get to a vision:

- **Why 1:** *Why is that important?* Because we exist to enable our businesses to be better off with us than without us.
- **Why 2:** *Why is that important?* Because if we can co-create TD initiatives that deliver real results, our company will be more successful.
- **Why 3:** *Why is that important?* Because if our company is successful, we can hire more people to expand our reach and impact.
- **Why 4:** *Why is that important?* Because by expanding our reach and impact, we can sell more products and services to more customers, which will lead to greater success and profitability.
- **Why 5:** *Why is that important?* Because the more products and services we sell to more customers, the greater impact we have on improving the experiences and lives of our customers.

So, Acme's vision statement might be something like "Improving the experiences and lives of our customers." Of course, you'd want to be as clear and specific as possible, so explicitly describing how and who the customers are would make the statement more compelling and inspiring. A vision statement should not only help you understand the future state you are pursuing through your business, but it should also motivate and inspire your company's employees to ensure that everything they do helps the company realize its vision.

What's Your Vision?
1. Consider these questions when formulating a vision statement:
   o What would happen if the reason we exist was no longer present?
   o What does "done" look like?
   o What impact would remove the need for what we do?
2. Take a look at these examples:
   o ATD: "Create a world that works better"
   o Feeding America: "An America without hunger"
   o IACET: "A world that learns better"
3. Write your own vision statement or revise an existing one.

Values

Values are descriptions of behaviors that help individuals within your organization understand how to interact with those you serve and how to live your mission every day. While numerous behaviors are necessary for an organization to live its mission and achieve its vision, you should identify a brief list of five to 10 core values that really differentiate your TD function and inform people of the distinct behaviors that are necessary for both people and the organization to be successful.

Remember, there are two different types of corporate values—those that are aspirational and those that are actualized. Aspirational values are indicative of behaviors an organization wishes to achieve in delivering on its mission. They're not yet present, or at least not prevalent, in the organization's culture. Aspirational values express a desire for people in an organization to behave a particular way, with the understanding that doing so will result in the organization being true to its purpose and in pursuit of its vision. They present an opportunity for you to transform those values into actual ones through your initiatives.

What Are Your Values?

1. Consider these questions when formulating your values:
   o What behaviors are necessary to live our mission and achieve our vision?
   o What behaviors differentiate us from other businesses or organizations?
   o What behaviors are the most important for everyone to exhibit?
   o What behaviors will we reward?
2. Take a look at these examples:
   o United Airlines:
     » Diversity and inclusion
     » Safe, caring, dependable, and efficient
   o Samsung:
     » People
     » Excellence
     » Change
     » Integrity
     » Co-prosperity
   o Feeding America:
     » We strive for equity and work toward solutions to eliminate structural and systemic inequalities that contribute to food insecurity.
     » We listen with empathy and respect for one another, valuing individual experiences and feelings while treating people with kindness and dignity.
     » We collaborate and build community through partnerships founded on integrity and trust.
     » We take care of resources placed in our hands through the generosity of others—food, funds, community and member trust, and employee careers and well-being.
     » We act with swift and focused purpose, allowing room for mistakes while seeking continuous growth and learning.
3. Write your own set of values or revise an existing set.

Revamp Your TD Portfolio

Informed by your mission, vision, and values, you should have a clearly defined business model that outlines how the function creates and delivers value for the business. Many functions have a traditional business model that ranges from new-hire orientation to leadership development. These business models are typically organized into categories, such as in Table 3-2.

Table 3-2. Traditional TD Business Model

Category	Sample Content
Compliance	• Legal requirements • Regulatory agencies • Accreditations and certifications
Onboarding and new-hire orientation	• Company history • Mission, vision, and values • Strategic plan • Culture • Employment policies
Personal enrichment	• Physical and emotional well-being • Financial wellness • Hobbies
On-the-job training	• Technical skills • Functional skills
Development and enablement	• Interpersonal skills • Technical skills

Although these five areas are the most common, in an effort to position the TD function to be more strategic and to gain leadership support, you might consider reimagining your TD business model. A more valuable TD business model might focus on the categories that business executives consider. If you were to ask a CEO what criteria they use to determine if their business is performing well, they might respond that they consider profitability, customer acquisition, customer retention, employee experience, and revenue diversification. You could use their responses to help shape a new business model for talent development that prioritizes those areas and aligns talent development initiatives to delivering those results. An alternative business model might look like Table 3-3 (on the next page).

Such a business model promotes the strategic alignment of your work to business success. Within each of these categories, you can conduct needs assessments at the macro-, meso-, and micro-levels (more on these levels in chapter 5) to identify initiatives that would maximize your contributions to the business. Read on for considerations about how you can reimagine five common initiative categories.

Table 3-3. An Alternative TD Business Model

Category	Determining TD Initiatives
Profitability	Examples of initiatives to ensure profitability of the business might include: • Sales training • Business process improvement training
Customer acquisition	Examples of initiatives to support the business in expanding into new markets and attracting new customers might include: • Language immersion programs (for employees to be able to communicate in new languages in new markets) • Brand fidelity training
Customer retention	Examples of initiatives to ensure the business retains its existing customers might include: • Customer service training • Active listening training • Conflict-resolution training
Employee experience	Examples of initiatives to improve the employee experience might include: • Leadership development training • Management training • Culture-building workshops • Team development training • Performance management systems
Revenue diversification	An example of an initiative to assist the business in diversifying its revenue sources might include: • Research and development

Compliance Training

Compliance training may be handled by a legal department or another business unit, but in many businesses, it's part of the talent development portfolio. Initiatives in this category are compulsory and must be completed for a person or a company to comply with an established requirement. While many compliance courses can be very beneficial to businesses by mitigating risks, they tend to be the least desired among learners. People generally don't like to be forced to participate in training. Because compliance training often touches everyone in a business—from the most entry-level position all the way up to the CEO, it can become the face of the TD function. If compliance programs are monotonous, lengthy, and unenjoyable, they can turn people off talent development.

Therefore, I highly recommend that if TD functions include compliance training programs in their portfolio they give it the attention and resources it deserves because it can make or break others' perceptions of the value the TD team contributes to the business. Further, consider customizing compliance curriculum to the business to make it as relevant, practical, and useful as possible. Focus on how it helps the business rather than emphasizing that it's required or that employees may be punished for not completing the program.

For example, if your business processes credit cards and you're required to administer an annual security awareness (sometimes known as PCI, or payment card industry) training course, use that as an opportunity to make sure all employees know how much money and what percentage of revenue comes from credit cards and how serious the company is about protecting sensitive customer data as part of its brand promise. This commitment leads to brand fidelity, which hopefully contributes to customer retention and acquisition, which leads to increased revenues, which leads to increased profits. Consider how profound that is: Rather than requiring security awareness training because the business must demonstrate its compliance to accept credit card payments, reframe the perspective so that it's clear how important it is for employees to behave in ways that help the company be more profitable. For TD functions that aren't responsible for compliance training, this could present an opportunity to improve learners' experience while also demonstrating value to the business.

Rather than requiring security awareness training because the business must demonstrate its compliance to accept credit card payments, reframe it so that it's clear how important it is for employees to behave in ways that help the company be more profitable.

Onboarding

Onboarding includes new-hire orientation at the enterprise level, as well as induction at various other levels in the organization. For example, the finance department might have a new-employee training program, while the accounts payable team may have a different one that is specific to its function.

When talking with TD professionals, I often hear that new-hire orientation is viewed as a necessity rather than a strategic activity. To counter that perspective, I offer my own experience. As an entry-level training specialist at the beginning of my TD career, one of my numerous responsibilities was organizing, scheduling, and leading new-hire orientations for all new employees at all levels. This meant I was effectively the door greeter, welcoming everyone in all jobs in all functions and disciplines to the organization. I became the face of the TD and HR unit (because our TD function was part of the broader HR team). As someone who was intrigued by the business and understood the importance of the organization's history, vision, values, strategic goals, and desired outcomes and impact, I learned everything I could so I could share that knowledge with my new colleagues. Beyond wanting to provide a shared understanding of the organization, I wanted them to feel impressed by the organization they chose to share their unique talents with.

While this was important to me as part of establishing a favorable employee brand (which wasn't a hard sell, given that the organization was mission-driven and not-for-profit), I quickly learned I was doing something else unintended but welcomed: I was becoming the friendly face of approachability for the HR team. When a new hire had a question about time off, they came to me. When a new hire had a question about benefits, they came to me. When anyone needed something, they came to me—not because I had all the answers, but because they saw me as helpful and knew I would find the answers for them. I credit this reputation for my success and elevation, eventually all the way to the top of the HR team as the chief human resources officer (CHRO) and head of global people and talent. Little did I know back then that research would eventually support the fact that new hires' experiences during the onboarding process is a leading factor in employee retention. The Brandon Hall Group found that a great onboarding experience could improve employee retention by 82 percent (Moloney 2022).

So, for TD functions responsible for new-hire orientation, I urge you to make it an extraordinary experience for everyone at all levels. One of the greatest aspects of that experience was that, while I was in an entry-level position, I got to interact with new colleagues at all levels, including executives in the C-suite. This was helpful in building relationships with business leaders throughout the organization. I was seen as someone who was there to help, and more important, as someone who cared so deeply about the organization and its success that I took the initiative to understand the business so I could proactively offer my assistance in ways they may have never imagined someone in HR could.

Personal Enrichment

Personal enrichment includes programs that address people's physical and emotional well-being, financial wellness, and hobbies. While it may seem atypical to include non-work-related programs as part of a TD function's portfolio, offering people opportunities to address life situations removes burdens that might otherwise detract from their work performance. Employers need to encourage employees to show up as their whole selves—their authentic selves. People can be messy. We're not just workers who perform a job. We're sentient beings who experience myriad emotions. We have thoughts and feelings that affect how we behave. We experience pain (emotional and physical) and joy. We experience anxiety and worry. We can become impaired by our fears to the point that it affects our ability to perform. Employers must accept and acknowledge that performance deficiencies aren't always caused by a lack of knowledge, skills, or abilities. In fact, in my experience as a people leader, many performance challenges are caused by impairments to capacity or motivation.

For example, an employee who is typically a solid performer may have performance issues when they experience financial troubles at home, which could be brought about by any number of things like paying for college, caring for elderly parents, buying a home in a good school district, or paying off medical bills. When we worry about the future, our mental capacity to focus can be diminished. And if worrying keeps us up at night, lack of sleep can compromise our physical capacity to perform. When our emotions negatively affect both our mental and physical capacities simultaneously, the likelihood of experiencing performance difficulties is increased. So, while personal enrichment programming may initially seem irrelevant and perhaps even inappropriate for a TD function to offer, it can be instrumental in providing much needed support and relief. Focusing on people as their whole selves demonstrates the importance an employer places on people, and that in turn can have a tremendous impact on how employees think and feel about their employer. If people feel valued and supported, especially during moments that matter, they are more likely to be engaged and productive.

On-the-Job Training

On-the-job training addresses the competencies required to perform a job. While most employers expect to hire candidates who are qualified to perform a job because of their education and experience (which are the competencies employers *buy*), there are often competencies for which new hires must be trained. These could be equipment, technology, or company specific. Structured on-the-job training through TD initiatives "builds" these necessary competencies. At the team or function level, you can be instrumental in working with business leaders to ensure that any skills needing to be built rather than bought are adequately and appropriately addressed. You should collaborate with your talent acquisition team to ensure your organization's hiring practices attract and select the competencies necessary for business success, which minimizes the need to build skills versus buying them. Thus, on-the-job training focuses on those skills that are unique to the organization.

Development and Enablement

Development and enablement involves initiatives that help learners acquire new knowledge or skills or improve existing ones. These opportunities are generally longer term in scope than on-the-job training. While they may provide value right away, they're usually intended to develop learners for future success. Many initiatives in this category include hard skills (technology-related competencies) and soft skills (interpersonal skills that are people- and relationship-related competencies). Employees generally find this portion of the talent development business model most valuable. To the extent that you can provide development opportunities to employees that clearly align to career progression—and employees who build such competencies are promoted from within—the greater credibility you'll have among employees and managers alike. Building capacity and competency among existing employees is a strategic approach to ensuring the organization has the talent it needs to remain relevant and competitive in a volatile, uncertain, and complex market.

Present Your Case for a Revamped TD Function

In preparation for reimagining the TD function in your organization, consider the function's mission, vision, and values (and whether any part of your TD portfolio is misaligned) and understand the relative importance to the business of the seven factors we examined earlier, especially the role of people. To do that, start by conducting a needs assessment as if you were designing and developing curriculum. While there are many ways to conduct a needs assessment, consider using or adapting this approach:

1. Conduct a stakeholder analysis.
2. Conduct an internal environmental scan.
3. Conduct an external environmental scan.
4. Identify your business's competitive advantage.
5. Prepare your business case.

We will walk through each step for the remainder of the chapter, culminating in your proposed business case for a reimagined TD portfolio that better serves your organization's mission, vision, values, and competitive advantage.

1. Conduct a Stakeholder Analysis

Recall from chapter 2 that a stakeholder analysis helps identify key stakeholders who have influence over and interest in your business case, and who they may play an important role in establishing a TD function. Consider the following:

- Identify the roles (and the people in them) that would likely need to approve the establishment of a TD function in your organization. Who *owns* the decision? Will the CEO need to be involved? Will the CHRO need to approve? Who can approve funding for staffing, technology, tools, equipment, and space?
- Identify who holds power on the executive team. What is the power dynamic? Who has influence over the CEO or CHRO? Whom do you need to convince of the value of talent development? Who can help advocate for resources and funding?
- Identify executives and leaders you need on your side. Who can help others on the executive team understand the value of talent development? How can they help build allies among other executives?

- Identify business leaders at all levels who are known as good people leaders and would support and advocate for you.
- Identify "super-keepers" throughout the organization: employees who are so important to the success of the business that their loss would be detrimental.
- Identify an executive sponsor for your business case.

Use the stakeholder analysis power map (see "Strategy 3: Level of Interest and Influence" in chapter 2) to determine how to prioritize and engage each of those stakeholders.

2. Conduct an Internal Environmental Scan

You must thoroughly understand the business you support. Demonstrating such an understanding not only helps ensure that you put together a solid proposal, but it can go a long way toward establishing credibility with business leaders. Conducting an internal environmental scan includes reviewing documentation and interacting with leaders throughout the business. To do this, you might consider these activities:

- Review your company's mission, vision, and values.
- Review your company's strategic plan to see how many objectives would benefit from the support of TD initiatives.
- Talk with your HR team to learn about turnover and retention statistics.
- Review exit interview data to see how many employees indicated or commented that a reason for leaving was related to their growth and development or wanting more learning opportunities.
- Use employee engagement or opinion survey data to learn employees' thoughts and feelings about talent development at your company.
- Talk with your talent acquisition team or hiring managers to learn how many internal candidates apply for open positions and to understand if they are qualified.
- Talk with your finance team to learn how much money your company spends on external training and development programs.
- Talk with employees to learn about their experiences working for the organization. Perhaps, have them rank the seven factors we discussed earlier in the chapter.

- Talk with business leaders to learn about the challenges that keep them up at night. By offering a proposal for how you can address those issues, you might deliver the necessary sales pitch to win over their hearts and minds and turn them into TD allies.

3. Conduct an External Environmental Scan

Consider your organization's main competitors—either for customers and market share or for recruiting talent in the labor market. Find out whether they have a TD function, and learn about their business models and how they contribute to your competitors' business. Although creating demand for talent development within your organization should not be driven simply by your competitors having an existing TD function, in any business, it's important to always monitor what your competition is doing.

Defining competitors may seem intuitive but can be complicated. For example, Lions Clubs International might seem like Rotary International's biggest competitor because both are global humanitarian service-club organizations. However, market research conducted by Rotary found that its competition wasn't necessarily other membership-club organizations, but rather opportunities for ad hoc volunteering. Whereas Rotary club membership typically involves participation at weekly club meetings, volunteering at a more spontaneous cadence may be more appealing to civic-minded people. And rather than aligning with one organization that focuses on a plethora of humanitarian service issues, volunteers might choose to help build a house with Habitat for Humanity one month, participate in a walkathon for the Alzheimer's Association another month, and organize a food drive for Feeding America another month. So Rotary's competition is primarily organizations that offer engagement opportunities without perpetual commitment. And when it comes to talent, Rotary's competition includes not-for-profit and for-profit organizations and businesses. In fact, in a typical year, more than half of Rotary's hires come to the not-for-profit organization from a for-profit company.

One way to identify your competitors is by asking customers and employees a simple question: "If not [insert business or organization name], then whom?" I might ask members of Rotary clubs, "If not Rotary, whom would you devote your time and money to?" I might ask employees, "If not Rotary, whom would you be working for?"

Competition is not the only consideration when conducting an external environmental scan. You should also examine several other variables, including:

- **Technological advancements**—how people use technology, particularly how customers use (or wish to use) technology in conducting business.
- **Economic conditions**—how people spend their money. Are they spending or saving? How are interest rates affecting consumer behavior? Are markets performing well or waning? How are exchange rates? What is the current consumer confidence level?
- **Societal conditions**—what people focus on from a human, cultural, and social perspective. For example, many consumers care deeply about fair business practices, including the use of child labor or exploited labor, procurement of goods, and supply chain conditions.
- **Current events**—what is happening in the world that may have an impact on business? The global COVID-19 pandemic, for example, had a tremendous influence on consumer habits and behaviors, business-to-business transactions, and virtually all aspects of life.
- **Labor market conditions**—what the employment landscape is like. Is unemployment high or low? What is the average time to fill an open position? Does supply exceed demand, or does demand exceed supply? What is the average turnover rate for businesses, and how does your company's turnover compare?
- **Paradigm cases**—what are other respected companies doing?

To illustrate paradigm cases further, many years ago, I worked with my colleagues in finance to understand how much money our organization spent sending employees to external training opportunities and where they were going. We identified two major suppliers that we paid significant sums of money to each year. I set out to understand why employees sought opportunities from those training providers rather than seeking internal training opportunities. By surveying staff and conducting focus groups, I learned that employees preferred those training courses for several reasons:

- They provided opportunities for employees to step away from their day-to-day work to focus on learning new knowledge, skills, and attitudes (KSAs).
- They brought people from multiple industries and businesses together to learn from one another, providing an opportunity to learn from peers outside the business.
- They perceived that completing courses from these vendors was helpful for building their resumes. The vendors' brand recognition and certificates of completion were tremendously important to employees.

We wondered what our organization could do to compete with those conditions and set out to replicate them. We created branded certificate programs. We intentionally included employees in various functions from across the business to bring people together who might not otherwise have a reason to collaborate. We created experiences that felt more like ones they would encounter from those vendors. Through further research, we learned that both training providers were accredited by International Accreditations for Continuing Education and Training (IACET), so we prepared a business case to have our organization's TD function accredited by IACET to demonstrate to our employees that the caliber of training they would experience internally was on par with what they might receive externally. The business case was approved.

4. Identify Your Company's Competitive Advantage

The market is full of competitors who offer similar products or services. Consumers decide which businesses to patronize, and in doing so, they consider the value proposition the business they ultimately choose offers them, which is essentially that business's competitive advantage.

The most prevalent value propositions for consumers—and competitive advantages for companies—include:
- **Quality**—offering products and services that are reputable and reliable, oftentimes providing consumers with a certain cachet. For example, luxury brands work hard to gain consumer confidence in the craftsmanship and longevity of their products so that buyers are willing to pay premium prices for their brand in exchange for having

greater peace of mind and even social status. Brands that focus on this competitive advantage include Apple, Louis Vuitton, and Starbucks.

- **Low cost** (sometimes called "cost leadership")—offering products and services at the cheapest price possible for turning a profit; this strategy generally requires volume selling, whereby the profit margin for each product or service is low in exchange for creating greater demand. Brands that focus on this competitive advantage include Walmart, IKEA, and Aldi.

- **Selection**—offering a variety of products and services that can be purchased together, sometimes even bundled. For example, fast-food restaurants continue to expand their menus to increase their average dollar per sale by upselling add-ons to meals. Most big-box retailers and grocery stores offer tremendous selections. Brands that focus on this competitive advantage include Amazon, Wayfair, and Overstock.com.

- **Convenience**—offering quick and easy-to-access products and services. While some companies with this competitive advantage are also low-cost leaders, others understand that consumers are willing to pay a premium in exchange for convenience. Brands that focus on this competitive advantage include Walgreens, McDonald's, and Hudson (found in most airports and transportation centers).

- **Service or customer experience**—offering consumers high-touch customer service or creating unique customer experiences. For example, many bridal gown retailers create entire experiences around selecting a wedding dress, complete with champagne. Pampering customers leads to brand loyalty. Brands that focus on this competitive advantage include Nordstrom, Hilton, and Qatar Airways.

- **Niche market**—offering products and services that are difficult to get anywhere else. Niche markets may be tied to a particular geography or shared value (such as fair trade), or target a particular demographic (such as children or women). Brands that focus on this competitive advantage include Lefty's the Left-Hand Store (left-handed products only), Untuckit (casual shirts that are not for tucking in), and Insomnia Cookies (late-night cookie delivery).

These qualities aren't mutually exclusive; they can coexist in any combination. Maybe while driving home, you notice that your gas tank is almost empty. Perhaps as you approach the next major intersection, you see multiple gas stations. You could choose the one that is most convenient (requiring only a right-hand turn, for example). Or you might choose one that also has milk and other staples you could buy while you're there (selection). Or maybe you choose the station you perceive to have better gas (quality). Or perhaps you go with the cheapest price (cost). Or maybe you're willing to spend a little more at a less convenient location because you really like the people who work there (service). Companies are always attempting to improve their value proposition for consumers by being intentional about their competitive advantage.

From a consumer perspective, you might have different value propositions for every product or service you consume, and even for each time you make a purchasing decision. For example, while fast food may be lower quality than a sit-down restaurant's, you might prioritize the speed of service (convenience) and lower price (cost). However, if you're taking a close friend out to eat to celebrate a major life milestone, you might choose a nicer place (quality) with upscale service that takes longer to prepare food—and you may enjoy the extended experience to socialize with your friend.

What is your business's competitive advantage? As part of your analysis, you must identify what differentiates your business. Let's look at an example of distinguishing what sets one company apart from its competitors.

There are many automobile manufacturers around the world, but Toyota stands out for consistently producing high-quality cars with few defects (lasting longer and requiring fewer repairs than American cars) while relying on fewer labor hours, less inventory, and less square footage than their competitors—so much so that in the 1990s, auto manufacturers around the globe recognized that Toyota was the competitor to beat.

Toyota has become the largest carmaker in the world, producing more cars in 2021 than any other auto manufacturer, and the second most profitable, bringing in more than $279.3 billion that same year (Confino 2022).

But considering there are only so many ways to manufacture cars, what set Toyota apart? Toyota attributes its success to empowering its people. It introduced a concept known as "stop the line," whereby any employee in any position at any level is empowered to stop a production line whenever they encounter a problem. When the line is stopped, production is not resumed until the issue is resolved and the root cause is identified. This concept has come to be known in Lean Six Sigma (an organized approach to improving performance by reducing waste and variation) as pulling the "Andon Cord," which for Toyota is literally a rope that anyone can pull. What I find most fascinating is that Toyota's management does not view this as an employee right, but an obligation. Employees are expected to stop the line when they know something is wrong.

While quality is certainly a prominent focus for Toyota, the thing that sets it apart from all other car manufacturers is the importance, trust, and expectation it places in every employee to be stewards of quality by requiring them to stop the line to address a quality issue. Other automobile manufacturers restrict the ability to stop their manufacturing lines to managers. Therefore, Toyota's culture and people are their competitive advantage.

To determine your company's competitive advantage, talk with people you identified in your power map to learn their perspectives on these questions:

- How do we define success for our business?
- What would make our business more successful?
- What do we do better than our competitors?
- Why do consumers choose us?

5. Prepare Your Business Case

Once you've identified your stakeholders via the power map, conducted an internal environmental scan (including the roles that people and culture play), conducted an external environmental scan, and determined your company's competitive advantage, you should compile the information into a business case to pitch to your company's executives. If you want your business case to be read, it should be short and to the point. It should focus on the prospective benefits of the talent development solution and the implications for not approving the proposal.

A business case should be composed of several items:

- **A description of the business challenges** that the business case will address
- **Identification of potential solutions** to the challenges

- **Recommendation of the proposed solution** from the list of potential solutions that you believe makes the most sense for the company (that is, it offers the highest probability of addressing the challenge, it is doable in terms of required resources, it is likely to be approved, and so on)
- **Accounting of the people and resources that will be required if the solution is adopted**, including staffing, space, equipment, technology, and budget
- **Timeline for implementation**

Your organization may have a template for such business proposals. If not, you might ask a business executive or an HR leader if they can share examples of business cases that have been used in your company, particularly those that were approved.

Summary

Gaining business leaders' buy-in takes work. Necessary work. Part of that work is uncovering and accentuating what makes your company successful and what sets it apart from competitors. Knowing your competitive advantage and understanding what role people play in it can position the TD function to collaborate with business leaders in very meaningful ways. Helping business leaders understand the importance of having a compelling mission, a shared vision, and guiding values all help to shape organizational culture.

Most organizations have a mission, vision, and values. Your TD function should too, and they should be aligned with those of your organization. But your TD function should also ensure that your organization's mission, vision, and values accurately capture the need it exists to address. They should also inform your TD business model. Revamping an existing TD business model is a great way to ensure you're positioning your organization for success. Presenting your case for a revamped model is a great way to build rapport and establish credibility with business leaders.

Chapter 4
Develop Your Business Acumen

You need to grow accustomed to speaking the language of business rather than the language of the TD profession if you want to prepare meaningful learning experiences that influence your company's success. You will need to regularly incorporate measurement and evaluation into your work. You'll need to propose, negotiate, set, monitor, and evaluate various metrics and targets that help tell the story of how successful your TD initiatives are, and hence how successful the business is. This may take you out of your comfort zone—which is both understandable and necessary—but you'll be surprised how accessible it is with the steps I outline in this chapter.

Speak the Language of Business

More than 7,000 languages exist in the world, but there is a single, universal language of business, and it's *not* English. It's *money*—not necessarily dollars, but whatever currency is relevant and valuable. Stories of business successes and failures are told using money—how much was earned, how much was spent, how much was invested, and how much was lost.

Most business executives speak this language, and to successfully work with them, it's imperative for us to relate to them by speaking it too, rather than the lingo of our profession. The TD field, on the other hand, has its own language that we learn and use to establish mutual understanding. When we speak to one another about the ADDIE framework, the five levels of evaluation framework, andragogy, adult learning theory, Bloom's taxonomy, or learning objectives, we recognize those terms and understand what they mean and their significance. As a profession, it's important we have this shared lexicon and understanding. But business professionals probably don't, and they might even be put off by our vocabulary.

Very early in my career, I worked with a CFO who thought I was "too academic" because I often used TD jargon when I presented to him and other business leaders. I thought I was demonstrating competence and conveying confidence but was actually alienating myself. I appreciated his perspective because it helped me realize that my ability to speak the language of talent development professionals was not what impressed business leaders; speaking the language of the business—*money*—was. The CFO didn't have any issue with my credibility or capabilities; he just didn't have time to decode what I was talking about. That turned out to be one of the most helpful, albeit unintentional, pieces of professional advice I have ever received.

> My ability to speak the language of talent development professionals was not what impressed business leaders; speaking the language of the business—*money*—was.

To demonstrate how TD initiatives add value and influence the business, you need to demonstrate how they contribute to increasing revenue, decreasing expenses, or both. It's as simple as that. No matter how complicated a business's financial statement, accounting boils down to two components: revenue and expenses.

Although it's uncommon for academic (undergraduate or graduate) and nonacademic TD courses or curriculum to focus on business acumen, the good news is that speaking the language of business doesn't require a degree in business, finance, or accounting. Although it's certainly ideal for all TD professionals who lead or wish to lead a TD department or function to understand basic accounting principles, it's not necessary to become a financial analyst to learn how to speak the language of business. In fact, we already do it all the time in our personal lives. Whenever we consider making a purchase, we intuitively consider its impact on our personal finances. We ponder the return on our investment: *Will the benefit I derive from this purchase be greater than the cost? How much is this worth to me? Is the trade-off for spending my money on this worth it?* We perform rudimentary calculations of how long it will take to pay off a purchase, and we act based upon the decisions we make about those calculations. This is precisely what business leaders do, only on a different scale and with different perspectives and context. Because we know how to do this in our personal lives, we can certainly apply these skills to the business world as well.

Undoubtedly, many TD professionals struggle to translate their work into the language of business, but it's a skill that many of us need to develop and cultivate. We tend to be people oriented rather than business oriented, and that is likely why we have a proclivity for focusing on the impact our programs have on people rather than the impact they have on the business—or the bottom line. But while we tend to naturally focus on one over the other, that doesn't mean we can't learn to become good at both. For example, you have an innate preference for which hand you use to write your signature, and it's well formed and comfortable for you. But with some practice, you can learn to competently sign it with the other hand too, even if you have to work longer to develop it into something that looks and feels natural. That signature from your nondominant hand will eventually become as legible as the one from your dominant hand. The same can be said when becoming business minded because it's a skill you can pick up with intentional practice.

> We tend to be people oriented rather than business oriented, and that is likely why we have a proclivity for focusing on the impact our programs have on people rather than the impact they have on the business—or the bottom line.

When we work with the business leaders we support, we want to make sure our presentations to them on how TD activities affect business results are as clear and concise as our understanding of how the same activities will change learners' behaviors. After all, the entire purpose of changing learners' behaviors is for them to *think, feel,* or *do* something differently than they did before, culminating in a desirable impact on the business. It is our responsibility to make that connection for business leaders. We simply can't afford to hope they're able to draw unarticulated and inexplicit connections between the two. Speaking the language of business ensures we can explicitly demonstrate how TD activities add value and deliver business results. That's how we win over the minds and hearts of the business leaders we support.

Ultimately, TD initiatives should be designed with the intention of changing learners' behaviors to achieve business goals and objectives, not simply for the sake of changing behaviors. Imagine if an initiative changed learners' behaviors, but didn't achieve a business goal or objective. Business leaders would probably not perceive the TD initiative to be successful because changing learners' behaviors is a means to an end. So, as TD professionals, we need to focus on how our work affects the end, not just the means.

Learn Your Business

To speak the language of business, you must understand the business you support as well as business leaders do. A relatively common criticism among business leaders about HR and TD professionals is that we don't understand *the business*. What we do understand, though, is how to develop talent. HR and TD skills are transferable to most businesses in most industries. If you can design learning programs for a retailer, you can design learning programs for a healthcare provider. Those are two very different industries, though, and just because your instructional design skills are transferable doesn't mean you should rely solely on them without learning about the business you support.

Being able to speak the language of business is necessary, but it's not the sole key to winning over business leaders. You must also demonstrate that you understand what they do, the challenges they face, and the external market conditions that affect them. You need to invest time and interest in learning about their business, and there are many ways to do so. Let's look at a few.

Research and Ask Questions

Beyond doing a general internet search, you should familiarize yourself with the information that all good business leaders should know. For example, you might ask people in your company:

- How did the business come into existence?
- When, where, and why was the business founded?

- Who founded the business?
- What is the business's mission? Why does it exist today? What purpose does it serve? What need does it satisfy?
- Whom does the business exist to serve? Who is its target audience? Why do they need the business?
- What are the business's core competencies? What does it do better than the competition? What is it known for?
- What are the business's primary sources of revenue? How much money does the business bring in each year?
- What are the business's primary expenses?
- What is the business's vision? What does the business hope to accomplish?
- Who are the business's biggest competitors?
- Who are the business's biggest or most influential customers?
- How is the business performing now? How does that compare with past performance? To competitors' performance?
- What are the biggest threats to the business?

You should also consult the company's mission statement, vision statement, values, income statements, and financial reports. As you read, write down any questions that arise. In fact, asking questions signals to business leaders that you're taking the initiative to learn more about the company, expressing your interest in it, and conveying that you care about it. While learning more about your company, you're also building rapport with business leaders and influencing their perceptions of you and the value you—and the TD department—can add.

As an HR professional, whenever I interview job candidates, I'm always interested in the questions they ask me because it gives me insights into what they know, not only about the job they're interviewing for, but also about the business in general. It helps me understand how their mind processes information and what they're curious about. All those things help me evaluate if candidates will be right for the job. As TD professionals, we should not only foster that curiosity throughout the employment life cycle, but practice it ourselves with the businesses we support, and model and reinforce the behavior for others.

Immerse Yourself

Yet another way to learn about your business is to immerse yourself in it. See if you can shadow others or jump in and do their jobs to experience the work firsthand. You could even talk to customers to learn about the business from a completely different perspective. While talking to customers might not seem like a common way to learn about your business, spending time with them in their environment can help create a broader understanding of how your company addresses their wants and needs and provide a more holistic perspective.

Understanding the business has become so important that more and more companies have decided to promote business executives into the role of CHRO because it's in the company's best interest for that person to know the business very well to ensure its people practices are conducive to enhancing and growing the business. Those business executives must then learn how to be good HR professionals. This practice raises a couple questions: Which is more important or valuable to the business—understanding the business or understanding human resources? And which of them is easier to learn?

Focus on Business Goals

Let's discuss the goals that most TD professionals are familiar with: course goals. As you've already figured out, they don't align with the language of business. Most often when TD professionals design and develop course curriculum, they focus solely on the goals of the course (how the course will affect learners) rather than on the goals of the business. Ideally, course goals should be business goals, and business goals should be expressed in terms of money. For example, the goal for a course to teach learners how to use a new software platform should specify how the course will affect the business, not learners' behaviors. The course is a means (change in learners' behaviors) to an end (impact on business results). Course goals should clearly articulate the end.

Reframe Your Course Goals

A simple internet search for writing course goals results in a plethora of guidance on using action verbs to articulate what learners will do differently after completing a course. This is what most TD professionals learn in both academic and nonacademic programs that prepare us for designing instruction. However, this is shortsighted because it doesn't help us expressly communicate to business leaders how TD programs will affect the businesses they lead.

A course intended to teach employees how to use a new financial management system might have a stated course goal: "Upon successful completion of this course, learners will be able to use the new financial management system." TD professionals might present this to a business leader sponsor of the training program as a performance goal for learners. To be clear, there's nothing wrong with performance goals that describe the desired change in learners' behavior, or the expected output of the training course for the learner. However, it is not a SMART goal (specific, measurable, achievable, relevant, and time-bound—more on this in the next chapter), and it stops short of articulating a desired business impact. It too narrowly focuses on what the learners will be able to do after they complete the course, and it fails to address how a business goal will be achieved. The goal as originally posed is really the purpose of the course, not the goal.

The good news is that existing course goals can be translated into business goals if they aren't already established. Business goals are what many business leaders refer to as key performance indicators (KPIs). They're measures of success. While not all KPIs are expressed in monetary value, in most cases, you can identify at least one KPI related to either revenue or expenses.

To reframe course purpose statements as business goals, or KPIs, you need to extrapolate the money. This is where things can get tricky, but rest assured, it can usually be done. Performance that may seem to be unmeasurable can be measured, so long as the cost of doing so is not greater than the value of conducting the measurement. One way to get there is by using the 5Y technique. The answer to each "why" question generally results in identifying a KPI that can be measured with money.

The example in the introduction illustrated how the high school principal reframed her course goal into a business goal. Table 4-1 demonstrates how the reframed course goal shows favorable financial impact. Although not all the metrics are measured in dollars, there is at least one measure of financial impact, which is helpful in getting business leaders to understand how TD initiatives can contribute to delivering results.

Table 4-1. Reframing Goals: Teaching Course

Original Course Goal or Learner Performance Goal	Reframed as a SMART Business Goal
Upon successful completion of this course, teachers will be able to prepare students for standardized state testing.	Upon successful completion of this course, teachers will be able to prepare students for standardized state testing, resulting in: • Improving student standardized testing scores by 15% in 2024, by 20% in 2025, and by 25% in 2026 • Increasing student retention by 10% in 2024, by 15% in 2025, and by 20% in 2026 • Increasing enrollment of new students by 5% in 2024, by 7% in 2025, and by 10% in 2026 • Reducing teacher attrition by 6% in 2024, by 10% in 2025, and by 14% in 2026 • Increasing state funding by 5% in 2024, by 7% in 2025, and by 9% in 2026

Let's look at a few more examples of reframing course goals into detailed business goals (Table 4-2).

Table 4-2. Reframing Goals

Original Course Goal	Reframed as a SMART Business Goal
Upon successful completion of this course, learners will be able to use the new financial management software.	Upon successful completion of this course, learners will be able to use the new financial management software, resulting in: • Enhanced efficiency by reducing processing time from two business days to one business day • Reducing errors by 90% • Reduced costs of $200,000 annually by reducing labor costs for processing time, errors, and error rework All measures will be achieved by April 30, 2024.
Upon successful completion of this course, learners will be able to explain product features and benefits to customers.	Upon successful completion of this course, learners will be able to explain product features and benefits, resulting in: • A 10% increase in sales revenue by December 31, 2024 • A 5% increase in average customer sales totals by February 28, 2025 • A 2% increase in customer retention by April 15, 2025
Upon successful completion of this course, learners will be able to prevent sexual harassment.	Upon successful completion of this course, learners will be able to prevent, identify, and appropriately address sexual harassment in the workplace, resulting in: • A 75% decrease in formal sexual harassment complaints by October 3, 2024 • A 90% increase in employees' psychological safety scores on the annual employee engagement survey by January 10, 2025 • A reduction of $50,000 of labor costs annually from spending less time conducting investigations • A reduction of $100,000 in legal fees for defending harassment cases

So how do you get to business goals from traditional course goals? For existing courses, you can start with traditional course goals that focus on what knowledge, skills, or abilities learners will acquire (learning objective) or changes in learners' behaviors (performance objective). You should be clear about how your TD courses are intended to change learners' behaviors.

The measures, metrics, and targets we use in the TD profession quantify outcomes. We track things like the number of courses provided, the number of learners who attend, and the percentage of successful completions. While these may be useful for understanding how well our initiatives are perceived, they fall short of helping us understand how our programs add value and affect the businesses we support.

Use the Logic Model to Understand How an Initiative Generates Value

You need to have metrics that measure results. Activities and capabilities should allow your business to enhance and strengthen its impact. A tool that is often overlooked in instructional design and talent development activities, but is relatively common in not-for-profit management for evaluating impact, is the logic model, which is a visual depiction of the relationship of variables from inputs to impact (Figure 4-1).

Figure 4-1. The Logic Model Process

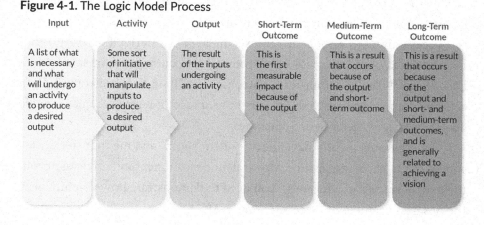

Input	Activity	Output	Short-Term Outcome	Medium-Term Outcome	Long-Term Outcome
A list of what is necessary and what will undergo an activity to produce a desired output	Some sort of initiative that will manipulate inputs to produce a desired output	The result of the inputs undergoing an activity	This is the first measurable impact because of the output	This is a result that occurs because of the output and short-term outcome	This is a result that occurs because of the output and short- and medium-term outcomes, and is generally related to achieving a vision

Figure 4-2 shows examples of how the logic model works.

Figure 4-2. The Logic Model Process Examples

Input	Activity	Output	Short-Term Outcome	Medium-Term Outcome	Long-Term Outcome
• Employee time • Wages or pay • Classroom space • Computers • Financial management system software • Training curriculum • Trainer	• Training on new financial management system	• Number of employees who completed training • Number of training courses offered • Number of training hours provided	• Improved knowledge of business processes • Decreased cycle time for accounting processes.	• Reduced recording errors • Increased efficiency	• Increase in number of customers • Increase in revenue • Reduced labor costs Increase in number of customers • Increase in revenue • Reduced labor costs

The logic model is a straightforward way to illustrate what is required to change behaviors and achieve results. It considers inputs, resources, activities, outputs, and outcomes, allowing users to understand how value is generated and measured.

If you accept that talent development initiatives are programs (sequences of activities) intended to change behaviors and produce desired results by moving from a current state to a future state, then you must first understand what the current state looks like. You also have to accept that maintaining the current state is insufficient for achieving a desired future state. So, to change the current state to a future state that is more conducive to achieving business goals and producing desired results, you need to determine what resources ("inputs") are needed to execute a TD initiative ("activity") that changes behaviors ("short-term outcomes") and culminates in achieving a business goal (the "medium-term outcome" and "long-term outcome"). Data collected for measuring the short-, medium-, and long-term outcomes provide guidance on how to monetize outcomes.

TD programs usually have more evident short- and medium-term outcomes, but to make the case for why a talent development initiative matters to the overall success of a business, you need to demonstrate how you influence the business in monetary terms (Figure 4-3).

Figure 4-3. Examples of Outcomes Translated to Money

Impact on Business	Language of Business
Increase in number of customers or clients	Increase in revenue (+US$)
Increase in average customer sale	
Increase in market share	
Increase in customer satisfaction	Increase in revenue (+US$) and/or decrease in expenses (-US$)
Increase in productivity	
Increase in efficiency	
Increase in quality	
Decrease in cycle time	Decrease in expenses (-US$)
Decrease in employee turnover	
Decrease in waste	
Decrease in labor costs	
Decrease in complaints	

While your TD initiative may be designed to increase the number of customers (converting shoppers to customers) or increasing the average customer sale, those are means to an end. In both examples, the outcomes will eventually result in an increase in revenue for the business, and that is what ultimately matters. Your work is to connect the dots for the business leaders you support so they understand how your initiatives manipulate inputs to produce outputs that are intended to result in short-, medium-, and long-term business outcomes.

Summary

TD professionals need to build business acumen and speak the language of business—money. Doing so requires investing time and effort into learning about the business you support. Understanding your company helps you understand what your colleagues do, and knowing that provides important context about the learners for the TD initiatives you create.

Reframing course goals as business goals that include measures, metrics, and targets helps TD professionals and learners understand what TD initiatives are intended to accomplish beyond simply learning new knowledge, skills, or attitudes. Logic models can help visually illustrate how your TD initiatives create value for the business.

PART 2

THE EIGHT-STEP EVALUATION-FOCUSED INSTRUCTIONAL DESIGN FRAMEWORK

The second part of this book focuses on approaching talent development initiatives from a business perspective by narrowing how you define success. Proactively identifying business needs and articulating business challenges using the language of business helps clarify how you can and will add real value. Course goals are business goals, and to ensure general understanding with your stakeholders, you'll learn how to write your business goals so that they are specific, measurable, adaptable, realistic, and time-bound and rely upon measures, metrics, and targets. Establishing your measurement criteria before designing and producing your initiative will set it up for success. Explore how to measure the consequences of your TD initiatives using five levels of evaluation: reactions, learning, behaviors or application, results or impact, and return on investment (ROI).

Chapter 5
Proactively Identify Business Needs

Now that you're fluent in the language of your business and you've built your function for success, you can focus on establishing initiatives that will generate real business value. In positioning yourself as a strategic partner with the business, you'll use the eight-step Evaluation-Focused Instructional Design Framework for designing meaningful learning experiences with evaluation in mind. I have used these steps both as a TD professional and as an instructor of graduate courses in measurement and evaluation for learning and development. This chapter examines steps 1 and 2, which involve identifying a business challenge and translating it into a business goal—the analysis phase.

Step 1: Identify a Business Challenge

By nature, TD functions in organizations exist to address challenges—either existing problems or future problems and opportunities. General human curiosity is evidence of our innate desire to solve problems and rise to challenges, such as solving mysteries and completing puzzles. The solution brings us closure and perhaps even joy. The sheer act of solving a problem for many people brings intrinsic satisfaction. And generally, solving a problem or accomplishing a challenge ends it, and we're hardwired to celebrate both successes and endings (graduations, retirements, and project celebrations). We declare victory, and we relish accomplishing something, until, of course, that challenge is quickly replaced by another. Then we repeat the process. Ultimately, TD initiatives assist businesses and organizations in bringing victory over business challenges. TD initiatives are a *means* to an *end*, and that end is a solved business problem.

TD initiatives are a *means* to an *end*, and that
end is a solved business problem.

Reframe How You Think About Problems

Language is extremely powerful, and the talent development profession is problem oriented—it influences not only how you do your work but also how business professionals and leaders outside talent development think about you, feel about you, and engage with you. Inherent in perceiving our function as problem oriented is that our function and our work get attached to something negative and undesirable. Given that your work intentionally changes behaviors, there must be merit in the presumption that real deficiencies exist with current behaviors. If that weren't true, there would be no need to change anything and no need for any talent development.

There is an opportunity for you to reframe your function's role—to go from being problem-oriented problem solvers to solution-oriented solution architects. Although you shouldn't create solutions without fully understanding problems and what causes them, this is an important shift in the way you and others think about what you do and the value you add to the businesses you support. When you reframe a challenge as a solution, you can completely change the way you think about, feel about, and respond to it, as evidenced with the word associations in Table 5-1.

Table 5-1. Word Associations With Problems and Solutions

Problem	Solution
Bad	Good
Negative	Positive
Deficiency	Opportunity
Demotivated	Inspired
Avoid	Welcome

In fact, I would take it a step further and suggest that TD professionals—and all employees of every organization and business—are not just solution architects but also inherently profit maximizers. Even employees of a not-for-profit need to ensure the financial viability of their organization.

I once suggested to a room full of TD professionals that we were responsible for profit maximization. I got a mixed reaction from the audience—a combination of agreement and bewilderment. One gentleman even interrupted me to suggest that he didn't become a TD professional to be focused on profits. He was adamant that his responsibility to his employer was to make sure its employees had the competencies they needed to be successful in their respective roles. He felt strongly that he was in the people business, not the profit business.

I completely understood his perspective, and he wasn't necessarily wrong. That's how many of us in talent development view our responsibilities. I would argue, though, that he was stopping short of acknowledging the true value he adds to his company. It may feel better to think you care more about simply changing people's behaviors than you do about increasing profits, but the reality is that TD initiatives for all nonprofit organizations and for-profit businesses exist to improve efficiency and enhance effectiveness. Ensuring that workers have the skills necessary to perform to their maximum potential should result in better, faster, or more productive performance. Perhaps it results in decreased waste, improved productivity, and greater efficiency. All of those lead to either increased revenue or decreased costs, which results in higher profits. So he wasn't getting to the language of business—money—as it related to his contributions to his company. Once he realized I wasn't talking about the TD function becoming a profit center and selling its services in a charge-back scheme, he understood that his work did affect profits.

How you think about the business you support informs how you understand your role in your company's performance and profitability, which influences what you focus on when designing, developing, and delivering initiatives, as demonstrated in Table 5-2.

Table 5-2. Evolution From People Business to Success Business

	Starting Posture	Reframed
Think	I am in the *people* business, responsible for helping others acquire new knowledge, skills, or abilities.	I am in the *success* business, and I share responsibility for the profitability and financial stability of the organization I work for.
Feel	I don't want any responsibility for the company's performance or profitability.	I value the opportunity to show how my work improves the company's performance and profitability.
Do	I focus my work on how it changes people's behaviors.	I focus my work on how it influences results and achieves business goals because of people's changed behaviors.

It may be intimidating or downright scary to think about having any responsibility for profitability, especially if you have never understood or appreciated that notion before. Accepting this comes with a great deal of accountability. It's much easier to only be concerned with how employees' behaviors have changed because of an initiative rather than the impact your work has on profits. This is traditionally the business's responsibility. But you're part of the business, so it's also your responsibility.

It's important to acknowledge that this responsibility is a shared one. We'll address this further in chapter 6, particularly the partnership between talent development professionals and business management as it relates to learning transfer that occurs on the job.

Collaborate With Stakeholders to Uncover the Root Causes of Symptoms

Once you reframe your mindset with respect to your responsibility to your organization, you're ready to explore the ways you can best help your company using step 1. It will come as no surprise after reading chapter 2 that you need to begin your pursuit in collaboration with your stakeholders.

Undoubtedly, this is difficult work, even for the most experienced TD professionals. In all aspects of life, we generally don't know a problem exists until we start to experience and pay attention to its symptoms. For example, you might notice you feel hot or cold. You might have a headache. You may be fatigued. All of these are problems, but what is causing them? It could be a virus or a bacterial infection. While you may want to mitigate or eliminate the symptoms, unless you have viable solutions for addressing the root cause (the virus or bacterial infection), the symptoms are likely to persist until the problem is eliminated.

Or you might notice that the temperature of your home is atypical for the season. That alone may be a problem. But is that *the problem*, or is it *a problem* that is also a symptom? There is a difference between *a problem* and *the problem*. *A problem* is an unfortunate circumstance that we experience because of *the problem*, which is the root cause. And how do you distinguish between them? I like to consider various perspectives of the problem:

- **Presenting problem**—the symptoms you first notice. For example, turnover among sales staff is high; it has typically been around 20 percent a year, but it has increased to 35 percent in the past 12 months.
- **Heart of the problem**—the actual business challenge. For example, high turnover affects revenue and expenses. Lost productivity from fewer sales staff has resulted in declining customer satisfaction scores, which has resulted in sales declining by $2 million in the past year. The cost of recruiting new sales staff has increased by 50 percent; therefore, costs are rising while revenue is declining.
- **Root causes of the problem**—the things discovered that are actually causing the heart of the problem. For example, sales staff don't feel supported and empowered to perform their roles to the best of their abilities; sales managers are so focused on the bottom line that they lose sight of the importance of ensuring an engaging work environment and a positive employee experience. Dissatisfaction with unreasonable expectations, distrusting managers, micromanagement, and noncompetitive wages has resulted in long-tenured sales staff resigning.

Dissecting problems in this way helps you tease out multiple facets of the issue to get to the language of business—money. The heart of the problem is typically the business problem that can be quantified in currency. And once the heart of the problem is identified, you can explore the root causes.

Many of your initiatives probably generate from these presenting problems, or the problems as they're presented to you. As part of conducting a needs assessment to analyze the problem, you'll seek to understand the root cause of a business challenge. For example, if a sales executive notices that

US-based sales are declining, you need to analyze what is happening to cause the sales to decrease. Declining sales, while a problem itself, is really a symptom; it's happening because of other variables. Perhaps additional competitors have entered the market. Perhaps consumers have less expendable income. Perhaps the sales team isn't sufficiently conveying product features and benefits in a compelling way that convinces consumers to buy the product. Perhaps the sales incentive program isn't enticing enough to motivate the sales force. Maybe it's a combination of multiple variables. What is critical, though, is to invest time and effort to fully identify and understand the root causes of the problem you're attempting to address.

When sorting through potential issues, you might need to help business leaders as they work to get to the heart of the problem. The 5Y technique is a useful tool because it helps drill down through multiple layers of symptoms.

A business leader may approach you with a presenting problem related to increased turnover in their business unit. Of course, excessive turnover alone is a problem. But is it the heart of the problem? Turnover is measured as a percentage of employees who separated from a company (involuntarily or voluntarily) relative to the average head count (by taking the starting head count for the period, adding the ending head count for the period, and dividing that number by two). Because turnover is not measured in currency, I would argue that it is not the heart of the problem.

Using the 5Ys, however, we can get to the true heart of the problem:

- **Why 1: Why is high turnover an issue?** Increased turnover results in lost productivity and decreased customer satisfaction.

- **Why 2: Why are lost productivity and decreased customer satisfaction issues?** Lost productivity because of employees quitting means that customers lose their connection (and trust) with existing staff and must establish relationships with new staff, which can be time consuming and frustrating for customers. Turnover also results in lost productivity, not just because fewer sales staff are supporting customers, but also because talent acquisition staff and hiring managers need to divert time, energy, and resources into recruiting.

- **Why 3: Why is it an issue if customers lose their connection with staff and have to establish relationships with new staff?** Customers get frustrated with the support they receive, and customer satisfaction scores decrease.
- **Why 4: Why is it an issue if customers get frustrated with the support they receive, and customer satisfaction scores decrease?** The more frustrated customers become, the less likely they are to place future orders. Decreasing customer satisfaction scores often correlate with compromised customer loyalty.
- **Why 5: Why is compromised customer loyalty an issue?** It's cheaper for a business to retain a customer than to attract a new customer. As a result of existing customers defecting from the brand, *the business has lost $2 million in year-over-year revenue.* Turnover and lost productivity also result in increasing replacement costs for the company, including the cost of advertising open positions, the cost of labor for talent acquisition professionals to review applications and screen resumes, the time investment required of hiring managers to interview candidates, the cost of training new hires, and the cost of lost productivity for not having a fully competent employee in the role. Replacement costs the company upwards of two times the employee's annual salary.

Notice how using the 5Ys helped us get to the heart of the business problem: US-based sales have declined by $2 million. That is the business problem we're attempting to solve. Once we understand that, we can then set out to understand the root causes.

As a result of the 5Y process, we determined that turnover is a symptom of a root cause. To the extent that you and the business leader agree on the heart of the problem, you can be focus on understanding what is causing high turnover. Let's use the 5Ys again:

- **Why 1: Why is turnover high?** Employees are frustrated with management.
- **Why 2: Why are employees frustrated with management?** Management doesn't empower employees to resolve customer issues.

- **Why 3: Why does management not empower employees to resolve customer issues?** Management doesn't trust employees to resolve customer issues sufficiently.
- **Why 4: Why does management not trust employees to resolve customer issues sufficiently?** Managers are primarily individual contributors who were promoted to oversee the work of others because of their longevity with the business rather than their qualifications and aptitude for leading others. As a result, managers have not been trained on the importance of autonomy and empowerment as they relate to job satisfaction and employee engagement.
- **Why 5: Why does the company promote managers primarily because of seniority rather than qualifications and aptitude for leading others?** Leadership assumes that high-performing individual contributors will make good people leaders and places an importance on how they performed in an individual contributor role.

So, in this example, the root cause appears to be *employee disengagement and dissatisfaction with management*. The TD initiative should address the root cause. Solving this issue should prompt a ripple effect that eventually affects revenues. Now you and your business leader need to collaborate on brainstorming solutions that might address the root cause and improve employee engagement and retention.

The presenting problem brought to you by a business leader may be a description of a symptom or actually form the basis of a hypothesis. Either way, the purpose of your engagement with them is to understand what you need to do to fully analyze the problem and determine what's causing it. Rather than simply accepting the symptoms or hypotheses presented to you by the business leader, you should do what a doctor would—collaborate with your patient (the business leader) to learn as much information as you need to form viable hypotheses you can then test. I use two approaches—business analysis and diagnostic analysis—to analyze presenting problems.

Strategy 1: Business Analysis

As part of step 1, conduct a business analysis. This means identifying the needs of the business (problems and opportunities) and the various requirements to address or achieve them. Needs generally fall into one of the following categories:

- **Normative needs** arise from a current state being inconsistent with a desired state or failing to meet existing norms. If an employer is required to provide compliance training on preventing harassment and discrimination in the workplace but is not, the need to do so is normative.

- **Felt needs** (often appearing as presenting problems) are identified based on what people think is needed or wanted. Felt needs generally represent people's wants, wishes, hopes, and desires. A business leader suggesting that you offer training on virtual meeting etiquette because of an experience they had might be a felt need. Or an individual who experienced an unpleasant interaction with another individual may present a felt need for sensitivity training.

- **Expressed needs** are identified by demand. They may be capacity needs. If a TD function offers two sessions of a course on belonging in the workplace, but the wait-list is longer than the enrollment list, there is an expressed need for more sessions and perhaps even more programing around belonging in the workplace.

- **Anticipated needs** are identified as being potentially necessary for proactively addressing future needs. A business that may eventually want to expand into the Chinese market might identify an anticipated need to understand business in China, perhaps even including language proficiency skills.

- **Comparative needs** arise when one group compares itself with another group and identifies disparities. A training vendor might compare itself with a competitor and learn that the competitor is accredited by IACET to issue continuing education units (CEUs). The vendor might identify a comparative need to also become IACET accredited.

- **Critical incident needs** arise when situations with significant consequences occur, and current conditions are insufficient. Workplace accidents may demonstrate a deficiency in safety practices and prompt a critical incident need to provide training on safety procedures (Burton and Merrill 1991).

Consider each of these categories, speak with colleagues and business leaders throughout your organization, and try to uncover where your business needs (symptoms) might lie.

Strategy 2: Diagnostic Analysis

Once you know your symptoms, a diagnostic analysis involves identifying why they exist. It consists of a root-cause analysis followed by a gap analysis.

A root-cause analysis means identifying what happened and why—the causes. Use these steps for conducting a root-cause analysis:

1. **Include the right people**. This should include people in the business who are closest to the problem.
2. **Define and understand the problem**. For example, if the problem is declining sales, make sure the people conducting the root-cause analysis are all working toward finding the causes of a mutually understood problem.
3. **Brainstorm possible causes** and form hypotheses by inviting those involved to postulate all the possible causes of the problem. As with all brainstorming exercises, this should be done without debate or critique—you want to try to think of all possible conditions that could be causing the problem.
4. **Review, evaluate, and prioritize possible causes** by having the individuals conducting the analysis go through the brainstorm list to identify the causes most likely contributing to the problem.
5. **Select top potential causes** from among the list of brainstormed possible causes.
6. **Form hypotheses for selected potential causes** to articulate how the cause might contribute to the problem.
7. **Test the hypotheses and look for causation or correlation** by collecting data, interviewing people, and conducting observations.
8. **Identify and agree on the causes of the problem.**

After the root-cause analysis, perform a gap analysis to identify the gap between the knowledge, skills, and attitudes that exist and those required to effect the necessary behavior change among learners to achieve business goals (Figure 5-1). Then determine strategies for closing the gap.

Figure 5-1. Gap Analysis

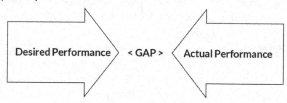

One way to conduct a gap analysis is to answer five questions relating to each step of the gap analysis. See Table 5-3 on the next page for an example.

1. **What is supposed to or needs to happen? (Expectation)** Before you can determine if what is actually happening is consistent with what is supposed to be happening, you need clear expectations of what is supposed to be happening. Some performance problems occur not because people are unable or unwilling to perform, but rather because there is no clear understanding of what is expected of them.

2. **What is actually happening? (Observation)** These observations generally occur on the job and assess actual performance.

3. **Is what is actually happening supposed to happen or does it need to be happening? Is it good or bad? (Evaluation)** Performance observation is compared with expectations to determine if performance falls below, meets, or exceeds expectations.

4. **Why is what is happening occurring? (Explanation)** Understanding what is causing actual performance and any gap between expectation and observation is important for understanding what needs to change to close the performance gap.

5. **What needs to change so that what actually happens is what is supposed to happen or needs to happen? (Calibration)** Or what needs to occur to reinforce and sustain performance that meets or exceeds expectations?

Table 5-3. Example of How to Use the Five Questions in the Gap Analysis

Step	Question	Example
Expectation	What is supposed to or needs to happen?	Employee is expected to type 75 words per minute.
Observation	What is actually happening?	Employee actually types approximately 50 words per minute.
Evaluation	Is what is actually happening supposed to happen or does it need to be happening? Is it good or bad?	The employee doesn't meet expectations, but through no fault of their own.
Explanation	Why is what is happening occurring?	Employee demonstrated their ability to type 75 words per minute in training. However, the equipment used on the job hindered their ability to perform to expectations.
Calibration	What needs to change so that what actually happens is what is supposed to happen or needs to happen?	Procure newer equipment or adjust expectation.

Certain analytics can be useful for these steps, as outlined in Table 5-4.

Table 5-4. Analytics for the Gap Analysis

Step	Analytics	Description
Expectation	Predictive	Analytics that help identify what could, should, or might happen, which are used to form the basis of expectations
Observation	Descriptive	Analytics that describe what is actually occurring
Evaluation	n/a	Although evaluation often leverages the results from analytics processes, it's a determination of whether there is a gap between expectations and what is actually occurring
Explanation	Diagnostic	Analytics that give insight into why something is or might be occurring
Calibration	Prescriptive	Analytics that provide guidance for what needs to change for performance to meet expectations

Let's take a more detailed look at each:

- **Predictive analytics** help determine what should or could happen. They are forecast measures of a potential future state. Predictive analytics are leading indicators because they model and predict future performance. For example, knowing that sales tend to increase in October, November, and December based on sales data over multiple years, and knowing the percent of increase in sales year-over-year, it would be reasonable to predict the sales performance for an upcoming October, November, and December. Predicted sales could inform the supply necessary to meet demand. It might also inform pricing, discounting, marketing, and promotion activity.

- **Descriptive analytics** help us understand what happened. They're measures of a current state. Descriptive analytics are lagging indicators because they measure what has already happened, or past performance. For example, measuring sales in October, November, and December describes actual performance. Descriptive analytics are useful data points for modeling prescriptive analytics.

- **Diagnostic analytics** help us understand why something happened. As part of understanding actual sales performance, you might compare sales performance data with other data points, such as customer satisfaction and product reviews. When those measures increase with an increase in sales, it might be difficult to establish causation (for example, an increase in customer satisfaction caused an increase in sales), but it might be reasonable to think there's a correlation (when customer satisfaction increased, sales increased). Knowing how correlations of performance data compare with other descriptive analytics can clarify why something occurs.

- **Prescriptive analytics** offer recommendations to drive future performance. Prescriptive analytics are important for businesses that use a data-driven approach to decision making. For example, a sales business might have a lead-scoring or lead-ranking scheme (built using predictive analytics) that helps it understand what activities indicate consumer behaviors consistent with the likelihood of converting interest to a sale. Sales businesses may consider data such as visits to certain webpages, reactions to marketing emails, and other behaviors that might express consumer interest. Predictive analytics inform the sales business of what it needs to close sales and might indicate which consumer segment to target with further marketing efforts.

Articulate Findings in the Language of Business—Money

Whatever process you use to differentiate among presenting problems, hearts of problems, and root causes (and the symptom problems they create), you must collaborate with business leaders so there is shared understanding and buy-in for any potential solutions.

Once you mutually agree on root causes, you then need to articulate the heart of the problem using language that will get business leaders' attention. As previously acknowledged, most business leaders don't understand the jargon of the TD profession. They speak the universal language of business, so you need to reframe business problems in terms of money. Although money isn't the only thing business leaders are concerned with, it does normalize measures and presents them in a light that magnifies the problem.

For example, if an operations executive indicates that production is down 20 percent, the next question should be, what is that worth? The value of the problem depends in part on the specific item and the reason for the slowdown, among other things. But for simplicity's sake, let's say the cost to the organization is $750,000 annually. Now, the head of HR tells you that turnover of critical talent is up 20 percent from last year. The consequence of this loss can be expensive—opportunity, acquisition, development, and institutional knowledge. Given all these factors, let's say turnover costs the organization $1.1 million annually. When you reframe the problem in terms of money, you can clearly see the scope of the problem, as demonstrated in Table 5-5.

Table 5-5. Heart of the Problem in Terms of Money

	Performance	Cost to the Organization
Productivity	Down 20%	$750,000
Turnover	Up 20%	$1.1 million

Here is another example. When the heart of the problem is vague—like declining sales—it's hard to know how big of a challenge you're facing. But when it becomes "Conversion rates by members of the sales teams have decreased, causing US-based sales to decline by $2 million annually," that is certainly a challenge you can work with! Ultimately, reframing this problem into a business goal will help show you're solution oriented and can favorably influence the business through accomplishing shared and desired results. We will explore how to translate business problems into goals in step 2.

Proactively Assess Varying Levels of the Organization

When business leaders approach you with a presenting problem, it inherently results in you being reactive, even if you're proactive in working with them to uncover the heart of the problem. When you conduct assessments at every level of your organization and identify challenges without business leaders seeking your assistance, you position yourself as a proactive business partner.

The initial approach to identifying business opportunities can be either reactive or proactive (Table 5-6).

Table 5-6. Reactive vs. Proactive Needs Assessments

Reactive	Proactive
Talent development waits passively until approached by leadership, managers, or employees about needs for TD initiatives—offering "presenting" problems (and possibly even a proposed solution).	Talent development conducts a needs assessment on regularly scheduled (usually annually) and ad hoc timelines to proactively identify opportunities for initiatives to help the business achieve its goals and objectives.
Talent development then reacts to the request for assistance.	Talent development proposes to business leaders how it can contribute in meaningful ways to achieving strategic business goals by changing the way people think about, feel about, and do something—and ultimately changing their behavior in ways that result in a desired outcome.
When following a first-come, first-served approach to allocating people and resources, requests are usually added to talent development's portfolio of initiatives and delivered in the order in which they're received.	Talent development collaborates with business leaders to prioritize how TD initiatives can maximize achievement of goals and objectives.
Talent development either provides what the business leader requests or engages stakeholders to determine the root causes and viable solutions.	TD and business leaders agree upon the business challenges (the *what*) and the TD initiatives that people and resources will be devoted to (the *how*).
Talent development designs, delivers, and implements a TD initiative.	Talent development designs, delivers, and implements an initiative.

Consider you current situation at your organization or company. What would you estimate your mix of proactive and reactive work to be today? Use Table 5-7 to record your thoughts.

Table 5-7. Your Proactive and Reactive Work

Approach	Percentage
Reactive	
Proactive	
	100%

Both approaches require relying on stakeholders to assist with identifying root causes and strategizing possible solutions. When business leaders come to you with a presenting problem, it creates a reactive posture—you're reacting to a business problem identified by someone outside the TD function. This suggests that business leaders bear primary responsibility for identifying issues to bring to the TD function. Sometimes presenting problems are coupled with proposed solutions, and when that happens, it signals that business leaders may perceive talent development as order takers—they approach us when they have a need, and they *order* a solution they think will address the issue.

For example, a business leader may approach you with a concern about low morale in their business unit, which they see as the root cause for declining customer satisfaction. They might specifically request that you provide a solution intended to boost morale. But just as a doctor wouldn't simply prescribe a medication to a patient who asks for it, neither should you position yourself as a reactive order taker. You're unlikely to solve a morale problem without understanding what exactly is causing low morale.

I once had a business leader ask me to conduct a "motivation" training session for employees. Knowing you can't teach people to be motivated (generally, people choose to be motivated and act based on their thoughts and feelings), I needed to help the business leader understand the conditions that were contributing to low morale. In fact, providing motivation training to employees with already low morale would likely be tone deaf and backfire. Although the intention to address morale is good, the proposed solution would likely exacerbate the problem. Instead, collaborating with the business leader on the root cause of low morale would result in brainstorming and agreeing on a solution (or solutions) that may actually be well received by employees and result in improving morale.

Incidentally, it turned out that low morale was caused by people leadership by the management team in the business unit. Employees didn't feel valued and respected. They had little to no autonomy. Their work was routine and mundane. They had few opportunities to learn new skills or perform new work. So, it was not the employees who needed motivation training; rather, it was the management team that needed training on more effective interpersonal relationships and people leadership. The business leader had incorrectly assumed the issue was with the employees. Although the employees were the stakeholder group that exhibited the symptom, they weren't the root cause of the problem.

Working collaboratively with business leaders to help them clearly define business challenges (as we will explore in greater detail in step 2) and understand root causes builds trust, which gives you the opportunity to brainstorm solutions with them so that:

- You can better manage the expectations of business leaders because you agree the solution can address the business challenge.
- There is a shared understanding of what and how the initiative can contribute to achieving the business goal.
- Business leaders understand the people and resources required to implement a successful initiative.

For your TD function to be truly strategic and a valuable partner to business leaders, even when initiatives are created reactively as the result of a presenting problem from a business leader, it's imperative you identify stakeholders and work collaboratively with them to understand root causes.

In my experience, TD leaders feel compelled to give business leaders what they want. They may see the sheer act of a business leader approaching them for assistance as proof they're perceived favorably and are adding value to the business. That may be true. However, that thought may result in hesitating to challenge business leaders out of fear of alienation, and you may simply accept the presenting problem and even the proposed solution. How you think about your relationship with business leaders informs how you feel about them, which affects how you interact with them (Table 5-8).

Table 5-8. Reframing Your Relationships With Stakeholders

	Starting Posture	Reframed
Think	I want business leaders to perceive me as helpful, strategic, and adding value to their business units.	I am a business leader who happens to work in talent development, and it's my responsibility to proactively identify opportunities for talent development initiatives to have the greatest potential for achieving business goals because that is critical to the business's success.
Feel	I don't want to challenge a business leader or deliver a talent development initiative that differs from what business leaders request because I might appear uninformed, disconnected, unsupportive, and uncooperative. If I provide exactly what business leaders request, they'll be satisfied, whether the initiative solves the problem or not.	I don't want to apply limited resources to talent development initiatives that don't solve root causes and will not be effective, so the greatest value I can add is challenging and exploring root causes and collaborating with business leaders to identify viable solutions. Business leaders will only be satisfied with initiatives that assist in solving problems, so they care more about getting the *what* and the *why* right than they do about me delivering exactly what they requested.
Do	I will deliver the initiatives that business leaders tell me they need.	I may not deliver the TD solutions that are requested, but I will deliver solutions that are most likely to achieve business objectives.

Many TD functions are a combination of reactive and proactive. You need to be ready, willing, and able to assist with requests that come your way, and they will always come your way, no matter how proactive you become. You'll need to react to things like new compliance training requirements, updated information for new-hire orientation, and requests for more professional development opportunities.

However, in my experience, the more proactive you are, the more successful your TD unit and business will be. When business leaders experience you taking initiative and demonstrating a thorough understanding of the business, they will see you more as a partner than an order taker. That said, you can lose credibility and status with business leaders if you're not responsive to the needs they bring to you. You have to find the sweet spot of how proactive and how reactive you wish to be and what the business requires. Ultimately, how a business leader thinks about talent development informs how they feel about it, which affects how they interact with you (Table 5-9).

Table 5-9. Reframing How Business Leaders Think About Talent Development

	Starting Posture	Reframed
Think	Talent development does not understand the business.	Talent development is a partner and an ally that I can count on to assist in identifying business challenges and viable solutions.
Feel	For talent development to be helpful, they will do exactly what is requested of them.	If talent development is going to really help, they need to help uncover the root cause and identify viable solutions.
Do	I will tell talent development what is needed.	I will invite talent development to assist and collaborate on identifying the root cause and viable solutions.

To be proactive, TD functions might conduct needs assessments at three different levels: macro, meso, and micro (Figure 5-2).

Figure 5-2. The Levels of Needs Assessments

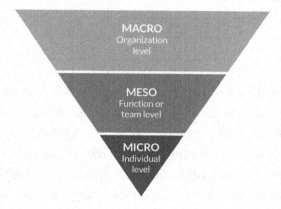

Let's explore each in more detail:
- **Macro**—the universal TD initiatives needed at the organizational level for all positions across the business, regardless of the level or function. Examples of macro initiatives might include privacy training or training on preventing harassment and discrimination in the workplace.
- **Meso**—talent development initiatives needed at the function or team level. For example, professionals in the HR function might need training on conducting investigations, while professionals in accounts receivable might require training in credit card processing.

- **Micro**—individual-level initiatives intended to improve the performance of one employee. This may take the form of a performance improvement plan for an employee who is performing below expectations or a professional development plan for an employee who shows promise and whom the business wishes to retain and prepare for higher-level positions in the future.

Consider the current situation at your organization. What would you estimate your mix to be today? What would you like those percentages to be for your organization? Use Table 5-10 to enter your estimated current and desired percentages for macro, meso, and micro levels.

Table 5-10. Your Macro, Meso, and Micro Mix

Approach	As Is	To Be
Macro		
Meso		
Micro		
	100%	100%

There is no ideal percentage mix—it really depends on the industry, business, and culture. In my experience, focusing on the meso level offers a great opportunity for you to address real business problems on a smaller scale while demonstrating the accomplishment of results that business leaders will share with other business leaders. The more that business leaders see successful results in other business units, the more likely they are to partner with you to assist with their own business units. Just as there is no magic formula for how reactive or proactive a talent development function should be, there is also no magic formula for focusing on the macro, meso, or micro level.

Now, after reviewing step 1 of the eight-step Evaluation-Focused Instructional Design Framework, what might the ideal mix of your future state look like in the next x number of months? Record your thoughts in Table 5-11.

What strategies could you leverage to move from your current state to this ideal future state?

Table 5-11. Future Mix of Reactive and Proactive

Approach	To Be
Reactive	
Proactive	
	100%

Step 2: Translate the Business Challenge Into a Business Goal

To shift from being *problem oriented* to *solution focused*, the next step is to translate the business challenge you've identified (the heart of the problem) into a business goal. If the business challenge is that US-based sales have declined by $2 million, a business goal might be "to increase US-based sales to $2.5 million by December 31, 2024." Notice that the goal not only endeavors to recoup lost revenue, but it also proactively attempts to exceed previous US-based sales by an additional $500,000.

The goal of the TD initiative is to contribute to achieving the stated business goal. It's not to put a certain number of learners through training, or even to impart new knowledge, skills, or abilities that change behaviors. Rather, the business goal informs the purpose of the TD initiative—to contribute to achieving an increase in US-based sales by $2.5 million in 12 months.

Business goals should begin with a verb to indicate a desired action. Review Table 5-12 for examples of business challenges that have been reframed as business goals.

Table 5-12. Business Challenges Reframed as Business Goals

Business Challenge	Business Goal
Declining sales: US sales have declined year-over-year by $2 million.	Increase US sales by $2.5 million by December 31, 2024.
Increasing waste and costs: The cost of processing each transaction has doubled from $8 per transaction to $16 per transaction because of delays and errors.	Reduce processing costs by 50% to $8 per transaction by June 30, 2024.

Table 5-12. (cont.)

Business Challenge	Business Goal
High turnover: Staff turnover has increased from 20% to 45% (100 employees a year to 250 employees a year), increasing replacement and onboarding costs by $6.375 million.	Reduce turnover to less than 20% and reduce replacement and onboarding costs by $6 million by December 31, 2024.
Desire to grow membership and revenue: Membership is at 1.2 million members, and dues revenues are at $73.3 million.	Increase membership to 1.4 million worldwide and increase dues revenues (through membership growth) by $12 million to $85.3 million by July 1, 2024.

Write Them as SMART Business Goals

The goals in Table 5-12 are very detailed, stating all the information needed to manage stakeholders' expectations and objectively know what success looks like, not to mention proving your business acumen. However, the most effective business goals are written as SMART goals, or goals that are specific, measurable, achievable, relevant, and time-bound. You may be rolling your eyes and thinking, "Here we go again with SMART goals," but I'm confident that being able to write goals that include all five elements is the best way to accomplish step 2.

Specific

Goals must be specific so that they're clearly understood. Anyone should be able to read the goal and know the desired result. For example, "lose weight" isn't a specific enough goal. Although it indicates the general desired change, it doesn't specify how much weight to lose or the timeframe in which to lose it. In fact, a goal stated that simply is technically satisfied if merely an ounce is lost, because the desired weight loss wasn't explicitly stated. It's important for business goals to be clearly articulated so everyone understands exactly what the goal is and how and when it will be monitored and evaluated. "Decrease employee turnover" might be a noble business goal, but it's not specific enough to know exactly what needs to happen to achieve it. How much of a decrease in turnover is desired? In what timeframe? Does turnover include involuntary separations (position eliminations or terminations due to poor performance), or is the business concerned only with voluntary separations (that is, employees who choose to separate from the company)?

Consider asking the following questions when crafting business goals: *who, what, where, when, why,* and *how?* The answers to these questions will help you create detailed business goals:

- **Who?** Which individuals or groups are critical to the goal? Who is responsible for the goal? Who is accountable for achieving it?
- **What?** What change are we trying to make? What was our starting point? What is our desired end point? How do we know when the goal has been achieved? What does "done" look like?
- **Where?** If applicable, which location or office is affected by this goal?
- **When?** When is the goal effective? What is the life or duration of the goal? At what intervals will we measure progress toward the goal?
- **Why?** What is the purpose for setting the goal? What will happen because of achieving the goal? What are the implications of not achieving the goal?
- **How?** What tactics will we employ to help accomplish the goal? What activities will the people critical to the goal be required to do?

Measurable

To state a business goal with adequate specificity, it must be measurable. You—or anyone else for that matter—must be able to quantify the goal. To be measurable, business goals need to have defined measures, metrics, and targets. All three of these interrelated criteria are important and necessary components of SMART business goals (Table 5-13):

- **Measure**—a variable that can be quantified and is expected to change because of accomplishing a goal. For example, a person wishing to become more fit or slender will likely measure either weight or waist size. So, weight or waist size become the measures for a weight-loss goal.
- **Metric**—a unit of measurement. Examples in business include dollars, yen, won, real, and percentages. A metric helps us understand how many or how much of a thing—and how the quantity of it is measured; it establishes a mutual understanding of how we (and others) will determine whether we have accomplished what we intended. For example, people who go on diets might use pounds, stones, or

kilograms as a metric for weight. Inches or centimeters might be used as a metric for waist circumference.

- **Target**—the ideal goal you intend to hit, or the value you expect to achieve. For example, people who go on diets usually have a target (or "ideal") weight they want to achieve. And if they hit their target, they know how they're performing.

Table 5-13. Weight Loss Measurements Example

	A	B
Measures	Weight	Waist Size
Metrics	Number of pounds lost	Number of inches lost
Targets	175 pounds	32 inches

It's vital to select measures, metrics, and targets that matter. What gets measured generally gets attention, so focus on measuring the right variables to determine how well you're performing toward the goal. Although it may seem overwhelming, it's typically easiest to brainstorm a list of possible measures, metrics, and targets, and then narrow it down to the right ones.

For several years, the Nature Conservancy, a global environmental non-governmental organization that exists to preserve nature, measured its success using two variables—bucks and acres—as shown in Table 5-14.

Table 5-14. The Nature Conservancy Measurements Examples

	A	B
Measures	Money ("Bucks")	Acres
Metrics	Money spent on buying land	Number of acres of land preserved
Targets	Varied by year	Varied by year

Even as the organization spent more money buying land and was preserving more acres each year, biodiversity wasn't improving. Species of plants and animals faced extinction. This was an issue even on the acres of land that the Nature Conservancy had purchased and preserved. Specifically, the organization purchased land near Schenob Brook, Massachusetts, with the express purpose of saving the bog turtles that lived there. However, the population of turtles there continued to decline. It became clear that the purchase of land where the animals naturally lived was not enough to save the species and protect biodiversity. As it turned out, it was polluted water from the surrounding lands that were not purchased that was affecting the turtle population. So bucks and acres were not the right measures for determining if the Nature Conservancy was successful in achieving its mission. After all, its goal isn't to acquire land.

In the mid-1990s, the Nature Conservancy changed the way it measured its impact. Having abandoned the bucks and acres measures, the organization spent years refining its metrics—at one point even having 98 metrics. Ultimately, the organization devised a more well-rounded, simplified approach to measurement and evaluation. It settled on three categories of measures: impact, activity, and capacity, as shown in Table 5-15 (Sawhill and Williamson 2001). It also set targets for each metric, but those are the organization's intellectual property and so not included here.

Table 5-15. The Nature Conservancy's Measures and Metrics

Measures		
Impact	Activity	Capacity
Metrics that demonstrate how well the organization is delivering on its mission: • Biodiversity health • Threat abatement	Metrics that quantify activities related to the organization's goals: • Number of projects initiated • Number of biodiversity sites protected	Metrics that ensure the organization has the resources necessary to achieve its goals: • Number of members • Amount of public funding • Growth of fund development • Market share

To help you determine what to measure, consider the following questions:
• Do we want to experience an increase (such as more revenue) or a decrease (such as fewer and lower expenses)? If so, by how much?
• How fast or slow (such as reduction in cycle time)?
• What level of quality (such as better products and services)?

For example, if the business goal is to increase sales revenue, ask, "How much of an increase is desirable, reasonable, and achievable by a specific date?"

Though we're focused on business goals, TD professionals regularly assist individuals with setting performance goals that align to business goals. In doing so, consider what each employee can or should do in their respective role—either individually or in collaboration with others—that is necessary for the business to achieve its goal. In other words, what does each employee need to do better, faster, or more of so the business is able to achieve its goal? Be very clear about the difference between a performance expectation and a performance goal (Table 5-16).

Table 5-16. Expectation vs. Goal

Expectation	A performance expectation is a defined requirement that an individual employee must achieve to fully meet expectations.
Goal	A performance goal is a motivational challenge to exceed performance expectations by doing something: • **Better**—improving quality • **Faster**—decreasing cycle time • **More**—increasing volume or output

Achievable

In addition to specific and measurable, a goal must be achievable. Although many people set stretch goals that are very challenging or nearly impossible to achieve, business goals should be attainable but not necessarily easily. For instance, it would be unrealistic for most people to set a goal to lose 100 pounds in one month. Not only is that unattainable (in most circumstances), but it would likely be unwise. So business goals need to be achievable. After all, you want to accomplish your business goals and show the business leaders you support the value you add by helping attain them.

How do you ensure that your business goals are reasonable and attainable? That requires you to find a sweet spot—a point where you stretch performance beyond what would have occurred without such a goal, but not so much that failure to accomplish it results in demotivation and defeat.

There are several ways to determine what is achievable. Previous experience (or accomplishments) is one of the best predictors of future performance. That's why job interviews rely heavily on behavioral interview questions that ask candidates to "tell me about a time when . . ." These questions elicit past performance to predict how one might behave moving forward. You might look back at what you were able to accomplish; consider if the results you attained were too easy, just right, or too difficult; and make changes as necessary. To continue our example, this is a common approach in setting weight-loss goals. Individuals who set out on a weight-loss journey usually have past practice to rely upon. They remember how much weight they were able to reasonably lose in the past using the same or similar tactics.

Another way to determine if a goal is achievable is to consider external benchmarks. This method gives you insights into what others outside your business have been able to accomplish. For a business goal around reducing employee turnover, you might rely on an external industry benchmark for comparable employees. In the early 2020s, turnover for nonprofit service organizations was about 19 percent, meaning that each year, about two out of every 10 employees would be new to the business. For an external benchmark for a weight-loss goal, you might ask your primary care physician what other people of comparable height, weight, body mass index, and overall health have been able to reasonably lose over a specific period.

You might also consider the performance of an exemplary employee. This is useful to know the extreme limit of what anyone might be able to do. If you're attempting to determine the best possible performance of a basketball player, you would probably consider Michael Jordan, a former player for the Chicago Bulls. It would be unreasonable to expect the average performer to demonstrate the same ability as an exemplar, but it can be useful in understanding what is realistic. Their performance can be used to manage an average performer's expectations by setting them at a lower, more achievable level.

If no data exists for determining achievable performance, you may have to run a test or pilot program to collect data to identify average expected performance. The sources for determining achievability are outlined in Table 5-17.

Table 5-17. Data Sources for Determining the Achievability of Goals

Source	Description
Previous experience (internal benchmark)	Rely on internal data from the past that informs what was possible and achievable.
External benchmark	Rely on external data from other businesses to inform what is possible and achievable.
Exemplary performer	Rely on the performance of the "best of the best" and establish a target reasonably below such performance that would be possible for an average performer.
Pilot program or test	When neither internal nor external benchmarks exist, you might have to test a goal to determine if it's achievable.

Relevant

A sound business goal must also be relevant to the nature and mission of the business. Indeed, it became clear that the measures and metrics the Nature Conservancy used were not sufficiently relevant to its mission and strategic goals. But using those measures and metrics resulted in staff aligning behaviors and actions with increasing the amount of dollars spent on land and increasing the number of acres of land preserved. As it turned out, those two measures were not the right ones for quantifying biodiversity.

So, for a business goal to be SMART, it must be relevant to the business, its mission, and its strategic objectives. If it's not, it shouldn't be a goal. In addition to aligning with the mission and strategic objectives of the business, goals should be important and matter to people. After all, one of most important reasons for setting goals is to provide everyone in the business with a clear understanding of what the business is trying to accomplish so that everyone aligns their work with making it happen. If people in the business don't think that a goal is relevant to the business or themselves, it becomes a collection of meaningless words rather than a framework for shared success.

Time-Bound

The difference between goals and dreams are that goals are finite and have a deadline. This is one of the most important elements of any goal—the duration of time necessary to accomplish it. Without setting a timeframe, it becomes impossible to know whether a goal has been achieved. For example, if you set a goal for yourself to save $1,000, you need to attach a deadline for the goal to be meaningful. If you set a start date of February 1 with the intention of saving $1,000 by November 30, you have 10 months to save the money, which amounts to $100 a month. Knowing the timeframe also helps us understand if a goal is achievable. Do you make $100 in expendable income that you can save each month over the next 10 months? If so, then that becomes a viable goal. If not, you need to reconsider the goal by changing the amount you will save, the timeframe in which to save it, or both.

Communicate Goals to Learners

Once you have written your SMART goals, you can clearly communicate them to learners when you launch the initiative. As TD professionals, we need to ensure that learners understand their role in how the business goal will be achieved and how the initiative will enable them to contribute to the goal in meaningful ways. This helps learners understand the significance of the initiative so they'll know they're not just there to learn new knowledge, skills, and attitudes, but rather to learn how they need to change the way they think about, feel about, and do something so that the business achieves its goal.

As TD professionals, we need to ensure that learners understand their role in how the business goal will be achieved and how the initiative will enable them to contribute to the goal in meaningful ways.

Whereas before we may have told learners, "We're here today to learn how to provide constructive feedback to build stronger relationships with employees," we might instead reframe it to, "We're here today to learn how we can contribute to Acme Inc's goal of increasing US-based sales by $2.5 million by in 12 months. One way to do that is to reduce employee turnover by 15 percent by improving the employee experience." Notice how the business goal becomes the course goal. This shift in mindset also helps remind you that all initiatives should be designed and developed to help the business achieve a business objective.

Summary

TD initiatives intend to solve business challenges. You must be able to correctly identify business challenges and should reframe them as business goals. Further, you must collaborate with stakeholders to uncover root causes. Using the 5Y technique can help you understand business challenges.

Analytics can be helpful in understanding what is expected to happen (predictive), what is actually happening (descriptive), why it is happening (diagnostic), and what needs to happen to remedy a performance gap (prescriptive).

Needs assessments (reactive, proactive, or a combination) help identify opportunities for you to add real value for your business. Needs assessments occur at three levels: micro (individual), meso (team, function, or department), and macro (enterprise-wide). Conducting needs assessments at different levels helps segment your TD offerings—some may be open to all employees or customers, some may be targeted to specific subset populations, and some may be intended for specific individuals.

Reframing business challenges into business goals is important for motivating and inspiring performance. When business goals are specific, measurable, adaptable, realistic, and timebound—SMART—they clearly identify what achievement looks like, removing subjectivity from determining if your programs contribute to business goals.

Chapter 6
Define Success

Different stakeholders may use different criteria to determine whether a training program was a success. Correctly and clearly identifying a business challenge is the most important task because it drives everything else. Once you and your business leaders agree upon a business challenge that is reframed as a business goal (steps 1 and 2)—but before designing, developing, and implementing an initiative—it's critical for you both to establish and agree upon success criteria. This makes up the new E_C phase of ADDIE reimagined. Steps 3 and 4 determine if learning is an appropriate strategy for achieving a business goal and establish success criteria that determine how you'll know if that business goal is achieved.

Your Lens for Evaluation (the Five Levels of Evaluation)

While there are many evaluation models we could adopt, a predominant and particularly helpful framework is the five levels of evaluation, which gives us a map for determining thorough evaluation criteria. One of the many things I appreciate about this framework is that it provides a structure for establishing measures, metrics, and targets to evaluate your initiatives from several different perspectives. It can be particularly useful to demonstrate how talent development initiatives change learners' behaviors during and after their participation in learning programs. This framework essentially addresses whether learners view learning programs favorably, if they actually learned through their participation, if their behaviors changed on the job, and how the business benefited. A downside is that TD professionals often use it as a summative framework (conducted at the end to summarize the effects of TD initiatives) rather than a formative framework (conducted throughout to influence the formation of TD initiatives). However, when used as I propose throughout this book, it provides a formative framework that shapes the design and development of learning initiatives.

Let's examine the levels and how you can use them to establish evaluation criteria to inform instructional design. Refer to Appendix B for more detailed strategies you can execute at each level.

Level 1: Reaction

Level 1 of the evaluation framework focuses on learner reactions. It measures their satisfaction with the coursework and instruction, their intention to apply the learning, and their perceptions of the learning. Level 1 instruments don't ascertain how behaviors (Level 3) will change after completing the course, and what results (Level 4) those changes will produce. To gain those insights, you must move beyond Levels 1 and 2 and evaluate at Levels 3 and 4.

Most Level 1 instruments are issued to learners at the end of a course. While this is an appropriate time to get a full understanding of learners' feedback, there are opportunities throughout a course to collect informal, ad hoc Level 1 reactions by asking for nods, claps, or other general feedback. These reactions are formative feedback for the instructor to make any changes necessary to remediate negative responses and reinforce positive responses.

In most cases, Level 1 evaluation instruments help you understand *how* learners feel, not necessarily *why* they feel that way, but Level 1 instrument items can be constructed in an effort to understand both; for example, a Net Promoter Score (NPS), which is outlined in Appendix B.

Level 1 instruments provide useful data about:

- **Instructor effectiveness**—whether the instructor contributed to the learning experience; whether the instructor was knowledgeable about the subject matter; whether the instructor was able to keep learners' attention; whether the instructor encouraged learner engagement and participation; and whether learners attribute their acquisition of knowledge, skills, and attitudes to the instructor.

- **Relevance of the curriculum**—whether the content was appropriate given the learner audience, whether the content was useful for the learners' roles, whether the content can be applied outside the training environment, and whether the learners believe the curriculum was appropriate for their success.
- **Appropriateness of materials**—whether the presentation, participant manual, jobs aids, and any other materials used were appropriate given the learner audience. In addition to understanding how valuable learners found materials during instruction, it may also be useful to find out if learners plan to use or consult the materials as references.
- **Learner loyalty**—whether learners are likely to recommend the initiative to others. This is an important measure because learners expressing their likeliness to recommend a course to others generally suggests they found it to be beneficial. In many ways, this is more useful than understanding how satisfied a learner is with a course because they could be satisfied but not recommend it to others. These measures might also prompt satisfied learners to recommend the course to others if they hadn't considered it. Measures of loyalty determine not just learner satisfaction, but how their satisfaction might manifest in their support of the course. It's one thing for learners to be asked to participate in a course by a superior; it is another to be encouraged to attend by others who have completed the course. After all, TD initiatives are strengthened by producing adopters rather than compliers.
- **Learners' intentions to apply new knowledge, skills, and attitudes on the job**—whether learners expect their behaviors to change on the job consistent with how their behaviors changed during the training program. Just as NPS measures learners' intentions to recommend or refer others, the expression of intention to transfer learning to the job is Level 1 (reaction) rather than Level 3 (behavior) because it measures intention rather than actual behavior.
- **How learners plan to apply knowledge, skills, and attitudes on the job**—beyond measuring learners' intent to change their behaviors

on the job, Level 1 utility items can also elicit data from learners about how they will apply their new knowledge, skills, and attitudes to the job.

- **Assessment of opportunities to apply learning on the job—** whether learners perceive they'll have the opportunity or ability to apply what they have learned to their jobs.
- **Assessment of changes to learners' knowledge**—learners can be asked to rate their knowledge of a subject before and after completing a course. These two data points can be compared to assess if there is any change in knowledge. Because these types of items don't actually prove a change in knowledge, they're not proof of learning (Level 2) or behavior change (Level 3). Rather, they're merely measures of learner perception. The benefit of measuring changes in self-perceived knowledge is that this Level 1 data can be correlated to Level 2 data, which can be helpful in understanding the extent to which learners attribute what they learned (Level 2) to their participation in the course. If there is little or no change to the ratings of self-perceived knowledge prior to and after attending a course, learners may have found no change in their knowledge. This suggests that learners don't believe participating in the course had any effect on their knowledge, skills, and attitudes.

So, for a TD initiative with a goal of increasing US-based sales by $2.5 million, you and your business leaders may agree that success from a Level 1 perspective is defined as:

- 85 percent of learners indicate that the instructor meaningfully contributed to their experience.
- NPS is at least +75.
- 100 percent of learners intend to apply what they learned to their job in the next 90 days.

Level 2: Learning

Level 2 instruments measure learning—learners' acquisition of new knowledge, skills, and attitudes—that occurred because of participation in the TD initiative. It should lead to learners applying behavior change on the job (Level 3) and contribute to achieving business results (Level 4). Without Level 2 data, you might not be able to demonstrate if or how learning contributed to achieving a business goal. Level 2 instrument items don't measure learners' reactions; feelings; estimations of their knowledge, skills, and attitudes; or intentions to apply learning to the job—those are all examples of Level 1 instrument items.

Level 2 evaluations are helpful for a few reasons:

- **Individually and collectively, they demonstrate if learners have acquired (or improved) their knowledge, skills, and attitudes** as a result of completing a course. From this perspective, Level 2 evaluations tell us how well learners did.

- **Individually, they identify learners who haven't successfully achieved the learning objectives.** Analyzing Level 2 instruments helps determine which remediation efforts might be helpful for which learners.

- **In aggregate, they provide insights into the effectiveness of a course** (including the instructional design, the instructor, and the materials). Patterns and trends in Level 2 data may indicate opportunities for improvement. For example, if 80 percent of learners incorrectly answer an item on a Level 2 instrument, that may indicate a potential issue with the item. Perhaps it was poorly written or the information wasn't included in the materials, wasn't part of the training, or was incorrectly covered by the instructor. Such a pattern would be worth investigating to find out why so many learners incorrectly responded to the item. From this perspective, Level 2 evaluations tell us how well *TD professionals* did analyzing the business need; designing the curriculum; developing the course activities, materials, and evaluation instruments; and implementing the course.

- **In aggregate, favorable Level 2 results can be useful in demonstrating the value the TD function adds to the business,** and could be useful in gaining greater support from business leaders for committing additional people, funding, and resources. This, of course, could increase talent development's capability to support the business and deliver even more results.

Level 2 evaluations are conducted during a training course or shortly thereafter. Generally, Level 2 instruments that measure learners' abilities to demonstrate their competency are conducted throughout a course when and where appropriate. Course activities aligned with learning objectives that culminate in someone assessing whether learners demonstrated their ability to apply new knowledge, perform a skill, or exhibit a changed attitude (such as quizzes, observations, role plays, and simulations) are Level 2 evaluations. Course activities that don't include some sort of assessment are simply exercises, not Level 2 evaluations. Level 2 instruments that measure knowledge (such as tests and exams) are usually conducted at the end of a course or soon thereafter.

It's possible for learners to demonstrate learning through Level 2 instruments, even if there is no subsequent application of behaviors (Level 3) on the job. This is precisely why collecting Level 2 data is critical for your initiatives. If no behavior changes are realized on the job, business leaders may incorrectly assume that training was ineffective and that learning didn't occur. Without Level 2 data, it would be difficult, if not impossible, to refute that assumption.

One of the challenges with Level 2 instruments is that, without assessing learners' entry knowledge, skills, and attitudes, it's difficult to isolate the effects of training programs. That is where Level 1 instruments can be useful. Learners can be asked to estimate the extent to which they attribute new knowledge, skills, and attitudes to their participation in a training program. Another way to isolate the effects of training on learning is using control and treatment groups, which will be covered as part of Level 4 evaluations.

So, for a TD initiative with a goal of increasing US-based sales by $2.5 million, you and your business leaders may agree that success from a Level 2 perspective is defined as:

- 98 percent of learners successfully complete a mock sales pitch exercise.
- 95 percent of learners pass a product features and benefits demonstration.

- 100 percent of learners pass the post-course assessment with a score of 90 percent or higher.

Level 3: Behavior or Application

Level 3 instruments measure the extent to which learners apply behavior changes learned in a course to their jobs (or from the learning environment to the application environment). These instruments also include measures that indicate the extent to which the work environment enables their use of the new knowledge and skills. Evaluating training transfer is important for understanding how learners use what they've learned after completing a course, with the understanding that behavior changes exhibited on the job (Level 3) lead to achieving desired business results or impact (Level 4). As with Level 2 instruments, Level 3 instrument items don't measure learners' reactions; feelings; estimations of their knowledge, skills, and attitudes; or intentions to apply learning on the job. These are all examples of Level 1 instrument items.

For you to prove behavior transfer on the job as a result of a TD initiative, learners must demonstrate that they acquired knowledge, skills, and attitudes during a course (Level 2). Thus, Level 2 evaluations should be conducted along with Level 3 evaluations for there to be a meaningful comparison.

Level 3 evaluations are important for a few reasons:

- **They help determine what learner behavior changes were applied on the job.**
- **They help you understand the extent to which learner behaviors have changed on the job.**
- **They encourage training transfer and application.** If managers and employees are aware that a Level 3 evaluation will be conducted, they may be more likely to make it happen.
- **They help assess the application environment,** particularly as it relates to how behavior changes acquired in a learning environment are encouraged or discouraged back on the job.
- **They help assess the impact of behavior changes on business processes, procedures, and operations** as a result of learners applying new knowledge, skills, and attitudes on the job.

Level 2 vs. Level 3 Evaluations

Level 3 evaluations are sometimes similar to the performance tests used in Level 2 evaluations—both measure changes in behaviors—but there are some primary differences:

- **Environment and conditions**—Level 2 evaluations measure the acquisition or improvement of learners' knowledge, skills, and attitudes, and occur during or relatively soon after learners have completed a course. Level 2 evaluations generally measure behavior changes in the learning environment under the observation of TD professionals. Level 3 evaluations measure the application of learners' behavior changes on the job. Level 3 evaluations measure behavior changes in the application environment—on the job—through observation (unknown to the subjects of the evaluation) and the insights of management, colleagues, direct reports, or customers. Research has shown that if subjects are aware that their performance is being observed, their performance will be generally more favorable than it would have been without being observed. This is known as the Hawthorne effect.
- **When the evaluation is conducted**—Level 2 evaluations are usually conducted during a training course or immediately after it, and Level 3 evaluations are conducted only after a training course.
- **Who conducts the evaluation**—Level 2 evaluation instruments are used by instructors, observers, and peers as part of Level 2 evaluations, while the same instruments may be used by supervisors, managers, learners (self-assessments), direct reports, colleagues, and customers for Level 3 evaluations.

So, for a TD initiative with a goal of increasing US-based sales by $2.5 million, you and your business leaders may agree that success from a Level 3 perspective is defined as:

- Sales managers attest that 95 percent of learners are using active sales skills gained during the training program.
- 95 percent of learners say that they are applying what they learned in the course when interacting with customers.
- 80 percent of surveyed customers indicate they witnessed the behaviors during their interactions with the learners.

Level 4: Results or Impact

Level 4 focuses on business results or impact. The eight-step Evaluation-Focused Instructional Design Framework proposed in this book requires that evaluation criteria be established prior to designing, delivering, and implementing training programs. These criteria are the result of your collaboration with business leaders during a strategy conference. In many ways, conducting a Level 4 evaluation is easy—the desired results have already been defined, and the evaluation itself often doesn't require constructing any evaluation instruments. While not always, you may rely upon documents, reports, and data that objectively establish whether desired business results were achieved by the set deadline.

It's important for you to attempt to quantify results in the language of business—money—when articulating business results or impact. Not all evaluation criteria or results can be translated into money, but when and where possible, it should occur as part of a Level 4 evaluation.

To demonstrate the impact of a program, you must isolate the effects of the training course from other factors. Remember, as you collaborate with business leaders to determine the percent of a business goal you agree training can achieve, you identify a number of initiatives beyond training that can contribute meaningfully to producing results. Several books describe different ways to determine the extent that training helped improve measures that matter. Three common techniques are control groups, trend analyses, and estimations (see Appendix B for more information).

So, for a TD initiative with a goal of increasing US-based sales by $2.5 million, you and your business leaders may agree that success from a Level 4 perspective is defined as:

- US sales increase by $2.5 million by December 31, 2024 (or 15 percent).
- Year-over-year US sales increase by 5 percent between December 31, 2023, and December 31, 2024.
- The executive leadership team has 85 percent confidence that learning contributes to 15 percent achievement of the business goal.

Level 5: Return on Investment (ROI)

Level 5 evaluates the financial return of a business's investment in a TD initiative by comparing the monetary benefits of a program with the cost of realizing them. Level 5 evaluation is instrumental in demonstrating your true contributions to business success, so you must understand what ROI means and how it's calculated. Being an astute businessperson with financial acumen is important for understanding any business, and it can be tremendously helpful in gaining the confidence, support, and partnership of business leaders.

This book doesn't use Level 5 evaluation to establish evaluation criteria for informing instructional design. However, Level 5 data is very helpful for completing step 3 of the eight-step Evaluation-Focused Instructional Design Framework because it can be used as predictive and prescriptive analytics. For example, you can use ROI to estimate the percentage that various solutions might contribute to achieving future business goals.

Level 5 evaluations depend on credible Level 4 results. From Level 4, it's a matter of annualizing the change in performance, converting it to money, and comparing the annual monetary benefits with the costs. Several metrics compare the benefits of an investment to the investment itself. For instance, return on equity compares net income with shareholder equity. Return on asset compares net income with the average of its total assets. These, as others, are important metrics and have a special purpose. The ROI measure that has the greatest utility is ROI reported as a percentage. This metric compares the annual net benefits with the fully loaded program costs (Figure 6-1).

Figure 6-1. The ROI Formula

$$ROI = \frac{Benefits - Costs}{Costs} \times 100$$

For more information on Level 5, please refer to Appendix B.

Step 3: Determine if Learning Is an Appropriate Strategy for Achieving the Goal

Once you and your business leaders identify a clear business goal, work with them and any subject matter experts to determine if learning is an appropriate strategy for achieving the goal. Remember, training is not always the most appropriate strategy. Before considering how training *could* be a solution, first consider *if* training *might* be a solution.

To illustrate, in the 1990s, a cleaning manager at the Schiphol Airport, in Amsterdam, the Netherlands, identified a business problem that was costing the airport money: excess "spillage" around the urinals in the men's restroom. There was clearly a performance gap among male airport patrons; the performance that was expected (no spillage) was not the performance that was occurring (excess spillage). But was training the right solution to address the performance gap? Should the airport have conducted training on how to use a urinal correctly? It is almost laughable to think about, and the answer is clearly no. Boys should have learned that psychomotor skill in their early formative years. Certainly, grown men do not need to relearn it. So what did the cleaning manager do? He formed a hypothesis: If he placed a fly decal in the urinal adjacent the drain, men might aim at the fly, preventing spillage. He tested the hypothesis and found that it worked. The airport reported an 80 percent reduction in spillage and an 8 percent reduction in janitorial costs (Ingraham 2017). It achieved its business goal of reducing janitorial costs and closed a performance gap without a training initiative.

Estimate the Value of Each Solution

Consider the sales goal we crafted in step 2: to contribute to achieving an increase in US-based sales by $2.5 million in 12 months. There may be several possible strategies for achieving that goal. For example, the company might introduce new products, adjust pricing, boost marketing and promotion initiatives, increase its sales force, implement an incentive program, and provide sales training. Ideally, the best way for a company to achieve a business goal is to consider multiple strategies. As part of our root-cause analysis in step 1, we determined that a lack of knowledge and skills (product knowledge and demonstrations) contributed to declining sales. So, a learning program would be an appropriate strategy. The question now, though, is to what extent. If we rely solely on learning as a solution, that goal may not be fully realized, but if we implement other strategies and estimate that learning will contribute 15 percent of the goal ($375,000), it becomes much more reasonable. So, if we guesstimate the other strategies, the mix of solutions looks like Figure 6-2.

Figure 6-2. Mix of Solutions

New products	30%	($750,000)
Pricing adjustments	5%	($125,000)
Marketing initiatives	15%	($375,000)
Increased sales force	25%	($625,000)
Incentive pay program	10%	($250,000)
Sales training	15%	($375,000)
	100%	($2.5 million)

With this predicted mix of solutions, we can manage business leaders' expectations about the extent to which learning will contribute to achieving the goal. Otherwise, they might assume that learning is *the* solution—100 percent. The challenge, of course, is that there is no magic formula to determine the percentages. We must get business leaders to agree upon a viable mix. As you learned earlier in the chapter when reviewing Level 5 evaluations, by conducting training evaluations that calculate a business's ROI, the business can build greater capability and capacity for accurately estimating and predicting the percentage that each solution might reasonably contribute to achieving a business goal. Again, ROI estimation data can be very helpful for collecting Level 5 data and provides internal benchmarks that can be used as predictive and prescriptive analytics.

In the example, TD professionals may bear responsibility for designing, developing, and implementing pertinent sales training for the sales team (measured by Level 1 evaluation), and for ensuring they acquire important sales skills (measured by Level 2 evaluation). In reality, management must encourage and reinforce training transfer on the job (measured by Level 3 evaluation) to increase sales (measured by Level 4 evaluation) that generate value (gross profit from the sales) to exceed the cost of the program (Level 5 evaluation). Further, you'll likely, and in fact *hopefully*, be involved in the other solutions as well. For example, if the company sends new products to market, you may need to conduct product benefits and features training for sales employees. And if the size of the sales force increases and talent development is responsible for new-hire orientation, that will require greater participation to onboard new employees.

Conduct a Strategy Conference With Your Business Leaders

You won't perform the solution estimations in isolation, so you'll need to conduct a strategy conference with your business leaders to arrive at an agreeable conclusion. Determining the extent to which training is a viable solution is more of an art than a science. There is no formula. This can be uncomfortable for TD professionals and business leaders alike. However, this process isn't so much about precision as it is about managing business leaders' expectations, building partnerships with them, and identifying ways in which a business can achieve its goals.

Once you identify and agree upon the business challenge and goal in steps 1 and 2, you can determine the TD function's potential contributions to achieving the goal by conducting a strategy conference with business leaders to brainstorm possible solutions and strategies. There are five steps to conducting a strategy conference:

1. **Identify** stakeholders relevant to the business goal who should participate.
2. **Invite** stakeholders to attend the strategy conference focused on the business goal.
3. **Brainstorm** possible solutions to achieving the business goal.
4. **Prioritize** the top five to 10 solutions by asking business leaders to rank them in terms of their potential impact.
5. **Negotiate** with business leaders on how well an initiative might contribute to the five to 10 prioritized solutions.

One of the primary reasons for the strategy conference is to manage business leaders' expectations so they don't think that the TD initiatives are the only contributors to goal achievement. You and your business leaders may begin the negotiation to determine the percentage they think each solution might contribute to achieving the goal.

The beauty of strategy conferences is that they:

- Mitigate the possibility for business leaders to dictate solutions.
- Mitigate the possibility for TD professionals to prescribe TD solutions.
- Encourage collaboration between the business and TD function.
- Create a sense of shared ownership over the business objectives.

- Help prioritize TD initiatives (including people, time, space, and resources).
- Provide a forum for business leaders to view TD professionals as strategic partners vested in the success of their business units.

When organizations first adopt this approach, they might not have the analytics to help predict the most likely percentage of the goal that each solution might address. As part of the negotiation, you should be able to articulate to business leaders how TD solutions can contribute based upon past experiences. The more that organizations use this approach, the more accurate they can become at predicting percentages.

You can also use strategy conferences with business leaders to assess business goals and help determine how the TD function should prioritize its workload.

If training is *not* the right solution for a business challenge (like the airport example), it's your duty to help business leaders understand why you believe it isn't a viable solution. You support far more than training solutions, and if you accept that all initiatives change peoples' behaviors to achieve a desired result, you must also accept there are initiatives other than training programs that can do so as well. For example, perhaps a sales organization introduces a new incentive pay program to reward salespeople for meeting or exceeding sales goals. Such a program is a TD initiative—it results in behavior change (more sales) and a desired result (higher sales revenues and profits)—but it may not involve any training.

Step 4: Determine What Successful Learning Looks Like

Steps 1 through 3 are all part of the analysis phase. Step 4 is the new E_C (evaluation criteria) phase of $AE_CDE_IDIE_E$ (ADDIE reimagined). You should now establish the evaluation criteria, or desired outcomes, to clearly define what successful learning looks like before developing the initiative. You'll use the five levels of evaluation as the framework for determining evaluation criteria.

Establishing evaluation criteria before designing and developing the learning program will help you ensure the learning activities align to achieving these targets and manage expectations around how successful the learning program will ultimately be. In addition, it will be much easier to design and develop the evaluation instruments (such as course evaluations, knowledge tests, and demonstration rubrics) that will be used for the last phase, E_E, which involves executing the evaluations.

For the TD initiative with a goal of increasing US-based sales by $2.5 million by December 31, 2024, through a strategy conference, you and your business leaders may collaborate on and agree to a definition of success from all four perspectives (Table 6-1).

Table 6-1. Evaluation Criteria

1. Reaction	2. Learning	3. Behavior or Application	4. Results or Impact
85% of learners indicate that the instructor meaningfully contributed to their experience	98% of learners successfully complete a mock sales pitch exercise	Sales managers attest that 95% of learners use active sales skills learned during the training course	US sales increased by $2.5 million by December 31, 2024 (or 15%)
NPS is at least +75	95% of learners pass a product features and benefits demonstration	95% of learners attest they are applying what they learned in the course when interacting with customers	Year-over-year US sales increased by 5% between December 31, 2023, and December 31, 2024
100% of learners intend to apply what they learned on the job in the next 90 days	100% of learners pass the post-course assessment with a score of 90% or higher	80% of surveyed customers indicate they witnessed the behaviors during their interactions with learners	The executive leadership team has 85% confidence that learning contributed to 15% achievement of the business goal

Once you and business leaders agree on strategies and the percentages of the solution they will contribute to—and if learning was identified as a strategy—you can create the evaluation plan. You will create the evaluation instruments later, during the design and development phases of the $AE_CDE_IDIE_E$ framework.

As part of an evaluation plan, you should indicate the levels of evaluation you will conduct along with the objectives and measures at each level—these become the evaluation items. Then identify the evaluation instruments you will use to collect data, the timing of data collection, the sources of data collection, and who is responsible for collecting the data.

Data collection methods and instruments vary, depending on cost, convenience, constraints, culture, and the utility of the findings using a particular instrument. Table 6-2 provides an example of different instruments you can use to collect data at the different levels.

Table 6-2. Methods of Collecting Data for Each Level

Method	Types of Data			
	Level 1	Level 2	Level 3	Level 4
Surveys	✓	✓	✓	
Questionnaires	✓	✓	✓	✓
Observation		✓	✓	
Interviews	✓	✓	✓	
Focus groups	✓	✓	✓	
Tests and quizzes		✓		
Demonstrations		✓		
Simulations		✓		
Action planning and improvement plans			✓	✓
Performance contracting			✓	✓
Performance monitoring				✓

Source: Phillips and Phillips (2015)

Data sources also vary, so go to the most credible ones who know about the change in performance. It has nothing to do with hierarchy in the organization. Rather, consider who is closest to the performance. Sources of data include:

- Learners
- Supervisors and managers
- Direct reports
- Peer groups
- Internal staff
- External sources
- Organizational records

Data collection occurs when you want to see the measures improve and when they have had an opportunity to improve. Level 1 and 2 data is collected during the program because that is when you need it. Level 3 and 4 data is collected when behavior change has likely occurred and business impact measures have had a chance to improve as a result of this behavior change. Sometimes this data is collected at the same time. The key is not to wait too long to capture Level 3 data so that you can make adjustments early. And don't wait too long to capture Level 4 data because the longer you wait, the harder it will be to attribute any improvement to the program and the less interested your stakeholders may be. Setting timing targets, like any target, can be tricky, so be thoughtful in your approach.

Responsibility for data collection varies. Typically, the TD professional facilitating the training course bears responsibility for collecting Level 1 and 2 data. Responsibility for collecting Level 3 and 4 data depends on the evaluation project. Sometimes the facilitator is involved, but much of the time a designated individual or team owns these higher levels of evaluation.

Figure 6-3 (on the next page) is a sample template you can use to plan your data collection strategy.

As you plan your evaluation, you might also develop a strategy indicating how you will analyze the data, specifically the Level 4 data that serves as the basis for the ROI calculation. This information will include the Level 4 measures, chosen techniques to isolate program effects on the measures from other influences, conversion of measures to money, cost categories, and intangible benefits. These issues are covered in more detail in many other books describing measurement and evaluation of talent development initiatives. Figure 6-4 is a template for planning the analysis for Level 4 and 5 evaluations (on page 127).

Once your plan is prepared, the evaluation instruments should be designed and developed in conjunction with the curriculum to ensure the curriculum can deliver the results for each level that will be evaluated.

Figure 6-3. Data Collection Plan Template

Data Collection Plan

Program: _____ Responsibility: _____ Date: _____

Level	Program Objective(s)	Measures	Data Collection Method and Instruments	Data Sources	Timing	Responsibilities
1	Satisfaction/Planned Action					
2	Learning					
3	Application					
4	Impact					
5	ROI	Comments:				

Source: Phillips and Phillips (2015)

Figure 6-4. Data Analysis Plan Template

	Data Analysis Plan						
Program: _____		Responsibility: _____		Date: _____			
Data Items (Usually Level 4)	Methods for Isolating the Effects of the Program or Process	Methods of Converting Data to Monetary Values	Cost Categories	Intangible Benefits	Communication Targets for Final Report	Other Influences or Issues During Application	Comments

Source: Phillips and Phillips (2015)

Summary

The most prevalent TD evaluation model includes five levels:

- Level 1 (reactions) is usually measured using surveys after a TD initiative.
- Level 2 (learning) is usually measured during or immediately following a TD initiative.
- Level 3 (behavior or application) is measured after a TD initiative in the application environment.
- Level 4 (results or impact) and Level 5 (ROI) are measured after some time has passed.

While most solutions to achieving a business goal involve talent development programs, not all solutions involve training (or learning). Training requires learners to acquire new or improved knowledge, skills, or attitudes and demonstrating their competency during the TD initiative. You need to identify if training is a solution, and if so, to what extent it might reasonably contribute to achieving a business goal.

You also need to collaborate with business leaders to determine what the achievement of business goals looks like and how your contributions will be measured. You can build a mutual understanding of what successful learning programs look like by establishing agreed-upon metrics, measures, and targets for Levels 1 through 4.

Chapter 7
Design Curriculum With Evaluation in Mind

Once you have collaborated with business leaders and agreed on evaluation criteria, you'll proceed to the design and development phases of the eight-step Evaluation-Focused Instructional Design Framework. Steps 5 and 6 are part of a content or instructional analysis. In these, you'll work alongside your business leaders to collaborate further and determine the knowledge and skills required for learners to change their behaviors in ways that will contribute to achieving the business goal. Then, during steps 7 and 8, you'll write course objectives and identify learning activities for each objective.

While you may think that it makes more sense to determine learning objectives first and then identify what knowledge, skills, and attitudes are required for learners to demonstrate proficiency in those learning objectives, I suggest the opposite approach. First, know the business goal. Then determine what's required of learners to contribute to achieving the goal. Finally, use that information to identify learning objectives. You don't want to risk identifying learning objectives that aren't required for accomplishing a business goal.

You'll notice that step 5 relates to knowledge and that step 6 relates to skills. There is not a discrete step identified for attitudes. This is intentional and consistent with the Think→Feel→Do Framework. You should consider what attitudes are necessary for ensuring learners are receptive to acquiring or improving the requisite knowledge and skills for achieving a business goal.

Step 5: Determine What Knowledge Is Needed to Achieve the Business Goal

If you determined in step 3 that learning is an appropriate solution for meeting your business goal, you should now consider what learners need to know (knowledge, which is part of the cognitive domain) to contribute to achieving that goal. You'll measure acquisition or improvement of knowledge with a Level 2 evaluation.

Ask yourself what knowledge learners need to acquire or improve upon to contribute toward achieving the business goal. You may decide on your own or during a strategy conference with business leaders. If you determine it independently, it should be reviewed and approved by business leaders because the course will be built around what you identify as requisite knowledge.

For example, a landscaping business's goal may be to increase sales of coniferous trees by 50 percent by June 1. For learners to contribute to achieving that business goal, they would need to acquire or improve their knowledge of what coniferous and deciduous trees are (definition), how to distinguish between and identify them (characteristics), and how to convince prospective customers of their features (size, growth pattern, or curb appeal) and benefits (ease of care or attracting certain birds).

Similarly, for a business wishing to increase its US sales by $2.5 million, TD professionals and business leaders may determine that its sales force must acquire (or improve) knowledge of product features and benefits (Table 7-1).

Table 7-1. Knowledge Required for Business Goal

Business challenge	US sales have declined year-over-year by $2 million
Business goal	Increase US sales by $2.5 million by December 31, 2024
Training as % of solution	15%
Knowledge	• Product features • Product benefits

Step 6: Determine What Skills Are Needed to Achieve the Business Goal

Next, you should determine what learners need to do or perform differently (psychomotor domain) to achieve the business goal, or what skills they must acquire or improve to contribute to achieving the goal. The acquisition or improvement of skills is measured by a Level 2 evaluation.

Ask yourself what skills learners need to acquire or improve to contribute to achieving the business goal. As with the previous step, you may decide on your own or during a strategy conference with business leaders. If you determine it independently, it should be reviewed and approved by business leaders because the course will be built around what you identify as requisite knowledge.

In the example of increasing US-based sales by $2.5 million, learners will need to acquire or improve their active listening skills, negotiation skills, and gaining-commitment or closing-sales skills. Identifying these skills helps inform the content of the learning program.

As with step 5, you should consider what attitudes might be necessary for ensuring learners are receptive to acquiring or improving the requisite skills for achieving the business goal (Table 7-2).

Table 7-2. Skills Required for Business Goal

Business challenge	US sales have declined year-over-year by $2 million
Business goal	Increase US sales by $2.5 million by December 31, 2024
Training as % of solution	15%
Skills	• Active listening • Gaining a commitment or closing the deal • Negotiation

Step 7: Use Needed Knowledge and Skills to Inform Course Objectives

Once the necessary knowledge and skills are identified, you can finally write learning objectives that adequately capture what learners need to do—remembering that the learning objectives need to support achieving the business goal.

Include the Three Components of Learning Objectives

American psychologist Robert Mager proposed that clear learning objectives should include three components:

- **Conditions**—a description of any circumstances under which a learner is expected to be able to demonstrate the skills indicated in the performance component

- **Performance**—a description of what the learner will be able to do (psychomotor skills)
- **Criteria**—a description of the measures, metrics, or targets that will be used to evaluate the learner's performance

For example, let's break down this possible learning objective: "With a hammer, six nails, and a piece of wood, the learner will be able to pound six nails straight into the piece of wood with 100 percent accuracy" (Table 7-3).

Table 7-3. Learning Objective Components

Component	Example
Conditions	Given a hammer, six nails, and a piece of wood
Performance	The learner will be able to pound six nails straight into the piece of wood
Criterion	100% accuracy

While noting the presence of all three components makes the strongest learning objectives, Mager offered that the inclusion of a condition or a criterion is not always necessary. However, a performance component is always required (Mager 1997). The performance component of learning objectives is drawn from learning taxonomies (see Appendix A).

Focus on Terminal Objectives Using Bloom's Revised Taxonomy

In terms of establishing objectives for TD initiatives related to the cognitive domain, instructional designers should focus on the highest-order level of Anderson's taxonomy (a revision of Bloom's taxonomy) that they can get learners to demonstrate as part of a training course. The levels are reviewed in Appendix A.

The highest-order learning objective is considered a *terminal objective*. All objectives that contribute to learners achieving a terminal objective are considered *enabling objectives*; they enable the fulfillment of terminal objectives. Terminal objectives are the purpose of the course—what learners will be able to do once they have successfully completed it—and enabling objectives are what learners must demonstrate they are able to do during the course. Enabling objectives are measured and evaluated as part of Level 2, and terminal objectives are measured and evaluated as part of Level 3.

The following example shows how instructional designers should employ Mager's performance-based learning objectives and Bloom's revised taxonomy to create suitable course objectives:

- **Course objective**—upon successful completion of this course, using evaluation criteria, learners will be able to create an instructional design package that will be approved by a business leader sponsor.
- **Objective level**—create.

A learner would demonstrate proficiency for that objective by exhibiting that they are able to perform the following:

- **Knowledge**—without the use of any sources (condition), the learner will be able to *recall* the steps of the ADDIE framework (performance) with 100 percent accuracy (criterion).
- **Understand**—without the use of any sources (condition), the learner will be able to *explain* how evaluation criteria are used to determine course objectives (performance) with 100 percent accuracy (criterion).
- **Apply**—collaborating with business leaders (condition), the learner will be able to *establish* evaluation criteria for what success looks like (performance) with 100 percent agreement by business leaders (criterion).
- **Apply**—given evaluation criteria (condition), the learner will be able to correctly *write* learning objectives that include conditions, performance, and criteria (performance) with 100 percent accuracy (criterion).
- **Analyze**—given a set of learning objectives (condition), the learner will be able to accurately (criterion) *explain* how course activities demonstrate that learning has occurred (performance).
- **Create**—given a set of learning activities (condition), the learner will be able to *create* an instructional design package informed by evaluation criteria (performance) that is approved by a business leader sponsor (criterion).

Because of the tiered nature of the cognitive domain taxonomy, we assume learners will be able to perform all the activities (enabling objectives) of the lower-order levels in order to demonstrate proficiency at the synthesis level (terminal objective). Again, terminal objectives are the purpose of the course, and enabling objectives describe the behavior changes necessary for learners to demonstrate proficiency of terminal objectives.

Write the Learning Objectives

You can use the learning domains to establish learning objectives for a course inspired by measurement and evaluation, and that take into account Mager's three components and terminal objectives (for the cognitive and psychomotor domains). To do so, you should assess the knowledge (cognitive domain), attitudes (affective domain), and skills (psychomotor domain) necessary for changing behaviors relative to conducting credible, meaningful evaluations (Table 7-4).

Table 7-4. Learning Objectives

Domain	Objectives
Cognitive (Think)	• Without the use of any sources, the learner will be able to *recall* the steps of the ADDIE framework with 100% accuracy (knowledge). • Without the use of any sources, the learner will be able to *explain* how evaluation criteria are used to determine course objectives with 100% accuracy (comprehension). • Given a set of learning objectives, the learner will be able to *explain* how course activities will demonstrate that learning has occurred (analysis).
Affective (Feel)	• The learner will *appreciate* the importance of measurement and evaluation in demonstrating results and proving value (responding; see Appendix A). • The learner will *embrace* that measurement and evaluation helps ensure the TD initiatives add value (valuing; see Appendix A).
Psychomotor (Do)	• Collaborating with business leaders, the learner will be able to *establish* evaluation criteria that express mutual agreement of what success looks like (application). • Given the evaluation criteria, the learner will be able to correctly *write* learning objectives that include conditions, performance, and criteria with 100% accuracy (application). • Given a set of learning activities, the learner will be able to *create* an instructional design package informed by evaluation criteria that is approved by a business leader sponsor (synthesis).

The example in Table 7-5 maps course objectives to the knowledge and skills identified in steps 5 and 6.

Table 7-5. Mapping Course Objectives to Identified Knowledge and Skills

Business challenge	US sales have declined year-over-year by $2 million	
Business goal	Increase US sales by $2.5 million by December 31, 2024	
Training as % of solution	15%	

		Course Objectives
Knowledge	Product features	Given a [*product*], learners will be able to demonstrate its use with 100% accuracy.
	Product benefits	Without the use of any sources, learners will be able to effectively communicate product benefits.
Skills	Actively listening	Without the use of any sources, learners will be able to effectively demonstrate . . .
	Gaining a commitment or closing the deal	Given a customer's narrative of needs, learners will be able to offer products or services that meet the customer's needs 100% of the time.
	Negotiation skills	Without the use of any sources, learners will be able to . . .

Step 8: For Each Course Objective, Design and Develop Learning Activities

Finally, you're at the last step of the Evaluation-Focused Instructional Design Framework. Now you get to design and develop your instruction. For each of the course objectives, determine appropriate learning activities that provide learners the opportunity to demonstrate proficiency of each objective (to support that learning has occurred). This will ensure that all learning activities align to course objectives (Table 7-6). At this time, you should also develop your Level 2 evaluation instruments.

Table 7-6. Course Objectives and Learning Activities

Course Objectives	Learning Activities
Given a [*product*], learners will be able to demonstrate its use with 100% accuracy.	• Mock sales pitch using product features • Product features knowledge test
Without using any sources, learners will be able to effectively communicate product benefits.	• Mock sales pitch using product benefits • Product benefits knowledge test
Given a customer's narrative of needs, learners will be able to offer products or services that meet their needs every time.	• Active listening scenario learner triads (customer, salesperson, and observer)
Without using any sources, learners will be able to . . .	• And so on . . .

When designing and developing course learning activities, you might consider the nine events of instruction framework proposed by American educational psychologist Robert Gagné. He says that courses should do the following for learners (Gagné, Briggs, and Wager 1992):

1. **Gain attention.** Start with a compelling way to gain learners' attention so they are compelled to contribute to achieving a business goal. Grabbing attention requires instructors to be mindful of learners' attitudes toward the company, the course, the content, and so on. The goal of step 1 is to ensure that learners are a captive audience ready to focus and learn. Setting the stage well can have a significant impact on how learners feel about the content, their participation in the course, and their readiness to learn, which are all part of the affective domain of learning.

2. **Inform learners of the learning objectives.** Once learners understand why they are participating and the business goal that they will contribute to achieving, the instructor should review the learning objectives and give an overview of the course learning activities that will be used to ensure learners are able to demonstrate proficiency of the learning objectives. Learners should understand why they are participating and what is expected of them as a result of their participation. It is wise to inform learners how learning (Level 2), behavior (Level 3), and results (Level 4) will be evaluated.

3. **Stimulate recall of prior learning.** A great way to help people learn is to provide opportunities for them to connect and associate new knowledge, skills, and attitudes with existing knowledge, skills, and attitudes. Course instructors should make every effort to encourage learners to build on what they previously learned in ways that help them clearly understand how what they are about to learn will enhance their existing competencies.

4. **Present new learning material.** Present new content in logical, coherent ways consistent with the learning objectives.

5. **Provide learning guidance.** Humans are social beings who often learn by observing others. To prime learners, instructors should demonstrate how to fulfill the learning objectives by illustrating

how to apply the new knowledge, perform the new skill, and exhibit a new attitude.

6. **Elicit performance.** Provide learners an opportunity to apply new knowledge, perform the new skill, and exhibit a new attitude. To ensure that learning has occurred during the course, Level 2 instruments should be used in conjunction with course learning activities so that the instructor, peers, observers, or others can assess whether each learner is able to accomplish each learning objective during the course.

7. **Provide formative feedback.** The Level 2 evaluation instruments should provide constructive feedback to each learner—reinforcing what they did well and detailing what they need to improve—with the intention of inspiring and guiding learning in accordance with the established learning objectives. From there, learners should be given opportunities to continue practicing until they perform to expectations. This feedback is considered formative feedback, which is intended to help shape and improve performance (Russ-Eft and Preskill 2009).

8. **Assess learners' performance.** To ensure that learners have mastered the learning objectives and are fully prepared to return to their jobs and change their behaviors in ways that will lead to achieving a desired business result, course instructors need to provide summative feedback, which clearly identifies how well each learner performed against each course learning objective, along with recommendations for further remediation and improvement if necessary (Russ-Eft and Preskill 2009).

9. **Enhance learners' retention and training transfer.** Course instructors need to set the stage for ensuring that learners retain what they have learned during the course and encourage learners to apply their new or improved knowledge, skills, and attitudes to their jobs. One way to promote retention and transfer is to inform learners that TD professionals will be monitoring and evaluating how they transfer what they have learned to their jobs by conducting a formal evaluation (Level 3). To prime learners,

instructors might even tell them when and how training transfer will be measured and evaluated. This is also a great opportunity to announce any reinforcement incentives that might have been agreed upon with business leaders (for example, an incentive pay program to encourage and promote training transfer).

Incorporating these nine events into your design and development will ensure that changes in learners' behaviors can be observed and evaluated, increasing the likelihood that the TD initiative will contribute to achieving business goals.

Summary

If training (or learning) is an appropriate solution for achieving a business goal, learners must acquire new (or improve existing) knowledge, skills, or attitudes. To ensure that your TD initiatives properly prepare them, it's imperative that you clearly define the knowledge, skills, and attitudes they'll need.

The curriculum should include learning activities that allow learners to demonstrate their acquisition (or improvement) of the relevant knowledge, skills, or attitudes during the course. All learning activities should be directly linked to course objectives, which should be directly linked to identified knowledge, skills, or attitudes.

Conclusion

For TD initiatives to be successful, the following must be true:
- They need to be aligned to business strategy or measures of business. Even compliance training can help an organization reduce its liability and improve its customer and employee experience.
- Business leaders must understand the importance of the TD initiative and how it's expected to contribute to business results or impact.
- TD professionals must accurately identify and adequately engage stakeholders throughout the instructional design process—including evaluation.
- Evaluation cannot be an afterthought; it needs to be a driving factor in the instructional design process.
- TD initiatives must result in changing learners' behaviors—how they think or feel about something, or do something differently than they did before their participation.
- Business leaders must ensure that conditions on the job (the application environment) are conducive to learners' applying their new knowledge, skills, and attitudes to ensure training transfer.
- Business leaders must hold managers and individual contributors alike accountable for training transfer.
- Business leaders, managers, and employees need to participate in TD initiative evaluations.
- TD professionals should learn from every TD initiative and apply their new knowledge to subsequent TD initiatives.

Once a TD initiative has been designed and developed using the eight-step Evaluation-Focused Instructional Design Framework, you can implement the learning activities and execute on your evaluation plan to determine if:

- Learning occurred during the course (Level 2)
- Behaviors were applied on the job (Level 3)
- Desired business results were achieved (Level 4)
- The benefits of the TD initiative outweighed the cost of providing it (Level 5)

This is how TD professionals make the case and deliver results!

Following the eight steps for designing, developing, and implementing TD initiatives (which contribute to business success by starting with evaluation in mind) will result in you demonstrating real partnership and value to the business. Not only do these steps help connect all ADDIE phases to the evaluation phase, but they also help set and manage expectations for business leaders around what learning can realistically accomplish. They create an approach that provides opportunities for you and your business leaders to partner together in the pursuit of delivering results.

APPENDIX

At the request of practitioners who've attended my presentations on this topic over the years, I wanted this book to be a one-stop primer for you to get adequate information that you can put to immediate use. Balancing practical application with the learning theories that inform the content, without asking you to read your way through an academic textbook, resulted in the inclusion of the following three appendixes. These go further into theory, as well as provide specific strategies for executing evaluation.

Appendix A. The Three Learning Domains
Appendix B. Applying the Five Levels of Evaluation
Appendix C. General Guidelines for Evaluation

Appendix A
The Three Learning Domains

Familiarity with the three learning domains is important for setting learning objectives that explain how people are expected to change the way they think about, feel about, or do something.

Cognitive Domain

The cognitive learning domain addresses how learners convert data into information and information into knowledge to influence how they think. This domain focuses specifically on the individual's ability to learn information with the intention of acquiring usable knowledge, comprehending information, applying what is learned to real-world situations, analyzing information, synthesizing ideas, and evaluating concepts. These levels comprise what is commonly referred to as Bloom's Taxonomy of Cognition—a tiered hierarchy that classifies these levels of thinking. In the late 1990s, Lorin Anderson, a student of Bloom's, revised the cognitive domain levels to *remember, understand, apply, analyze, evaluate,* and *create* (Figure A-1). This update changed the labels of the levels to verbs and swapped the order of *create* and *evaluate*, suggesting that the ability to create something from scratch (create, which Bloom called "synthesis") is a higher order than being able to evaluate something that already exists (Anderson et al. 2001).

Figure A-1. Anderson's Taxonomy: A Revision of Bloom's

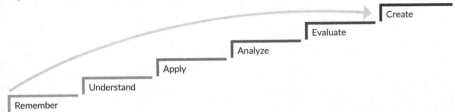

Let's explore each level in more detail:

- **Remember**—the ability of learners to remember and recall information through memorization, not necessarily with an understanding of its meaning. For example, a person might be able to remember that World War II ended in 1945, but they may not be able to explain why it ended or which countries were involved.

- **Understand**—the ability of learners to assign correct meaning and interpretation to information they acquired and can recall. The ability to provide context and explain a concept demonstrates a person's understanding of the information. For example, a person operating at this level would be able to articulate what happened in 1945 that led to the end of WWII or how sunlight hitting raindrops produces a rainbow, not just the fact that it does.

- **Apply**—the ability of learners to use information by applying it in a meaningful way. For example, if a baker knows that mixing flour, water, salt, and yeast makes bread, and they understand baker's percentages (the weight of each ingredient other than flour is calculated as a percentage of the weight of the flour), they can apply their knowledge and understanding to scaling the recipe to make more or less dough, and more or less bread, without changing the ratio of ingredients or affecting the bread's flavor and texture.

- **Analyze**—the ability of learners to deconstruct information to understand how the various parts make up the whole. For example, a person could document a business process using a flowchart with swim lanes (rows used to indicate who does what) to understand the order of steps in the process and who performs them.

- **Evaluate**—the ability of learners to judge the value or worth of an object, idea, or experience. For example, if a teacher wants to determine how successful they are at teaching, they must be able to critically examine their performance, its impact on their students, and the results it ultimately produces.
- **Create**—the ability of learners to put information together. For example, as someone reads a book or watches a movie, they're exposed to a plethora of information. As the plot starts to form, to make sense of the events unfolding, the reader or viewer must connect the dots by bringing disparate pieces of information together and making sense of them, not individually, but as a collective whole.

The six categories are stepped, or tiered. For a learner to perform at any one of the levels, they must also be able to perform proficiently at the preceding levels. One of the reasons I appreciate Anderson's update is that it suggests we must be able to evaluate before we can create, and that is the entire premise of this book: We must know how to evaluate a TD initiative before we create one.

Affective Domain

The affective domain focuses specifically on learners' attitudes or orientations. David Krathwohl proposed the Krathwohl Taxonomy, which addresses attitudes or orientations that shape our emotional responses and inform how we feel about subjects, objects, ideas, and experiences. The affective domain classification system is composed of the following five levels:
- **Receiving**—a learner's willingness to build awareness of ideas, values, and phenomena, and at minimum, tolerate their existence. Simple awareness requires a learner to be open to receiving information. Paying attention is an example of receiving.
- **Responding**—a learner's active participation in reacting to a subject, an object, or an experience. It starts when the learner takes an interest in the content being presented. Reacting is a form of responding, whether negative or positive, wrong or right. For example, if you make a declarative statement about something to someone who disagrees, you might reasonably expect them to respond by conveying

their disagreement. This behavior distinguishes between simply receiving and being apathetic to a given topic and responding to it. Responses may include agreement, disagreement, or further inquiry to learn more about the stimulus.

- **Valuing**—when a learner assigns meaning to or accepts ideas and appreciates phenomena so they're seen by others as valuing or embodying them. Learners behave in ways consistent with the beliefs they value, and others recognize and predict whether their behaviors will be consistent with their values. For example, if a colleague values the importance of time, they might always be on time to meetings and expect others to be as well.

- **Organization**—when a learner organizes different values and can reconcile conflict among them. This often involves comparing values, connecting like values, prioritizing values, and committing to values. For example, a person who loves animals and expects them to be treated humanely may also eat animal products.

- **Characterization by a value or value set**—when a learner has an established value system that influences and controls how they act or respond to situations and circumstances. Behavior is generally consistent and predictable (Krathwohl, Bloom, and Masia 1964).

Psychomotor Domain

The psychomotor domain focuses on learners' observable behaviors or actions. While there are multiple classification systems for this domain, I prefer to follow the taxonomy proposed by R.H. Dave (1975). Dave's taxonomy addresses physical movements and coordination. It includes five categories:

- **Imitation**—a learner's ability to observe the physical movements of another and mimic them. An example of imitation is when a person learning to line dance watches and copies the footwork of a lead line dancer until they memorize the dance moves.

- **Manipulation**—a learner's ability to perform an act or a series of acts after having observed or learned about them. An example of manipulation is when a person bakes a cake after watching a video of someone doing it or reading and following a recipe.

- **Precision**—a learner's ability to perform an act or a series of acts without requiring any assistance or feedback. An example of precision is when a person successfully performs CPR without any guidance.
- **Articulation**—a learner's ability to combine skills, correctly sequence them, and consistently apply them. An example of articulation is when a person learning multiple different brushstrokes and painting techniques combines them—with precision—to create a piece of artwork.
- **Naturalization**—a learner having mastered a high level of performance so the skills are rote, or second nature. An example of naturalization is when a person drives a car on a regular route without consciously thinking about or even remembering all the psychomotor skills that doing so requires. Using the turn signal is a psychomotor skill that a driver may not even be conscious of performing.

Appendix B
Applying the Five Levels of Evaluation

Chapter 6 reviews what each level of the framework means and why you might use it. This appendix details more specific strategies for executing each level. This isn't intended to be a comprehensive guide for understanding TD measurement and evaluation frameworks, constructing evaluation instruments, or analyzing and reporting evaluation data. Plenty of other books and resources provide greater insights into the mechanics of those activities. The following information is a general overview of the framework and how you can use it when establishing evaluation criteria to inform instructional design.

Level 1: Reactions

Level 1 focuses on learners' reactions. The usefulness of data collected by Level 1 evaluation instruments varies depending on what data is collected and how it's used. If Level 1 instruments collect data that isn't used in any meaningful way, there is little to no value in collecting it.

In most cases, Level 1 evaluation instruments help you understand how learners feel, not necessarily why they feel that way. But Level 1 instrument items—such as the Net Promoter Score—can be constructed in an effort to understand both how and why learners feel the way they do. To understand why learners feel the way they indicate on a Level 1 instrument without an open-ended option to explain their rating, or to learn about how learners intend to apply behavior changes on the job, you may want to conduct further evaluations. For example, you could conduct follow-up interviews or focus groups with learners who participated in a course that resulted in low measures of learners' intention to apply a new skill on the job to understand more about their course reactions.

Most Level 1 instruments are issued to learners at the end of a course to collect their reactions. Although this is an appropriate time to get a full understanding of learners' feedback, there are opportunities throughout a course to collect informal, ad hoc Level 1 reactions as well. These reactions are formative feedback for the instructor to make any changes necessary to remediate negative responses and reinforce positive responses. Examples of formative Level 1 evaluations include:

- **Nods**—responding to an inquiry by nodding; asking learners to nod their heads up and down if they understand or shake from side to side if they do not.
- **Show of fingers**—responding to strength of agreement or likelihood by a show of fingers; asking learners to hold up five fingers if they strongly agree, four fingers if they agree, make a fist if they're neutral, two fingers if they disagree, or one finger if they strongly disagree.
- **Clapping**—responding to strength of agreement or likelihood by clapping; asking learners to clap five times if they strongly agree or once if they strongly disagree. (Tip: Start with strongly disagree first so any higher-level responses don't drown out the lower-order responses.) Clapping can be used as an auditory indicator, using the volume of clapping to assess where learners are with the material. For example, you might ask, "Do we need more time, or are we ready to move on? If we are ready to move on, clap loudly!" and determine pacing based on the volume of clapping.
- **Stand or sit**—responding to an inquiry by standing or sitting; asking learners to stand if they understand or sit if they don't. These types of physical responses encourage people to move around, which can be helpful in maintaining participation and engagement. Learners who don't feel comfortable expressing that they don't understand content may not respond honestly, but anyone who remains seated can be asked what they don't understand. If they express that they were

not participating, it might be a good indicator that they do not fully understand a given subject.

- **Checking in**—asking learners questions to check in and soliciting open-ended feedback from those who wish to respond. Questions you might ask include "What about this resonates most with you?" "What is still unclear?" "Where are you stuck?" "What would you like to learn more about?" "What aha moments have you experienced?" and "Does this make sense?" When a learner answers one of these questions, you might follow up by using one of the previously described approaches.

If a learner shares that a certain portion of the content was confusing for them, you might ask all learners to use a show of fingers to understand if there is confusion among the whole group. If you see that several learners are still confused, you can adapt the session to clarify the content before moving on. It's better for you to address confusion during the session than to find out about it once the course is over. At that point, it may be too late to do anything about it for that particular group of learners.

Level 1 evaluations are helpful primarily for measuring learner satisfaction with and attitude toward learning, their intention to apply the learning, and their perceptions of learning. Let's review methods to reach each of these goals.

Learner Satisfaction and Attitude Toward Learning

Regarding measures of loyalty, a referral score often used in marketing is called a Net Promoter Score, or NPS. I find NPS measures to be more useful than many other Level 1 items because measuring an intention is more helpful in understanding what a learner might do than simply measuring a reaction. NPS was introduced in 2003 by Fred Reichheld at Bain & Company to move beyond measures of satisfaction and instead understand the behaviors that could result from satisfaction—detraction, apathy (passive), or promotion (Reichheld 2011). It's composed of two parts:

- **Rating**—learners are asked to rate (closed-ended item) how likely they are to recommend the course to others, which is an indirect way of measuring how learners feel (assuming learners would recommend a course only if they thought was meaningful in some way). This part of the item doesn't provide any insights into why learners feel the way they do or rated the item the way they did. NPS uses an 11-point scale (0 to 10) to measure how likely someone is to recommend or refer others to consume a good or service or patronize a company, with 0 being *least likely to recommend* and 10 being *most likely to recommend.*

- **Explanation**—learners are also asked to explain (open-ended item) the rationale behind their rating. For example, if a learner rated the item a 9, they are asked to explain why. This additional information provides context for why learners feel the way they do about the course.

An NPS measures only *intentions* to behave a particular way (Level 1), not actual behaviors (Level 3). NPS is also not useful for predicting behaviors. For this reason, some critics of NPS recommend abandoning it altogether, suggesting there is little correlation between a learner's intention to refer others and actually referring others. Yet another criticism of NPS is that training providers might incentivize respondents to rate the course favorably with positive experiences that don't necessarily result in their acquisition of new knowledge, skills, or attitudes. In an attempt to artificially manipulate NPS, training providers might focus more on eliciting a positive emotional reaction (for example, by providing a great meal), which might cause learners to feel favorably about the course ("I really enjoyed this"), which might cause them to do what the training provider wants (respond favorably to recommending the course to others—whether they actually end up doing so or not). While I certainly understand these criticisms and concerns, I still find NPS more useful than any other Level 1 item.

NPS categorizes learners based on their responses. Responders who rate the item 0 through 6 are considered "detractors," which means they're not only unlikely to recommend the item, but they might even actively deter others from using it. Respondents who rate the item 7 or 8 are considered "passive," which means they're essentially unlikely to detract or promote the item to others. Respondents who rate the item 9 or 10 are considered "promoters." They're the ones most likely to encourage others to consume the item or patronize the business. Once you analyze the NPS data and determine each category of responder, you can then determine your score. NPS is calculated by taking the percentage of promoters and subtracting the percentage of detractors. Table B-1 shows an example of NPS as a Level 1 instrument item.

Table B-1. NPS Example

Item: How likely are you to recommend this course to others? Please explain the reason for your rating.

#	Anchors	Respondents	%	#	%	Category
0	Not at all likely	0	0.0%	5	5.7%	Detractors
1		1	1.1%			
2		0	0.0%			
3		2	2.3%			
4		1	1.1%			
5		1	1.1%			
6		0	0.0%			
7		8	9.2%	28	32.2%	Passive
8		20	23.0%			
9		33	37.9%	54	62.1%	Promoters
10	Extremely Likely	21	24.1%			
		87	100%	87	100%	

The NPS is calculated by taking the percentage of promoters multiplied by 100 and subtracting the percentage of detractors multiplied by 100. Net Promoter Scores can range from −100 to +100. The NPS for Table B-1 is 56.4:

$$(62.1\% \times 100) - (5.7\% \times 100) = 62.1 - 5.7 = 56.4$$

In addition to the scores, respondents' explanations for their ratings are compiled as qualitative data and can be coded and reported accordingly.

What is a good NPS? There is no correct answer to that question; it's relative. Each industry may have a different interpretation of NPS scores. Reichheld (2011) believes that any score above 0 is positive because it suggests you have at least one more promoter than you do detractor. To determine a good NPS for your organization, collect enough baseline data to establish an internal benchmark that you can compare an individual course's NPS to. Once you define a desirable internal NPS, you can use that benchmark to determine goals for increasing it. As a rough frame of reference, I aim for an NPS of +70, which means removing an equivalent number of detractors from the total number of promoters (so if 82 percent of respondents are promoters, and 12 percent are detractors, the NPS is +70).

Recalling the discussion around ensuring goals are measurable (as part of being SMART), measurability requires goals to have established measures, metrics, and targets. For NPS, those might look like the ones listed in Table B-2.

Table B-2. NPS Measures, Metrics, and Targets

Net Promoter Score	
Measure	Likelihood to recommend to others
Metric	Numeric rating from 0–10, with 0 being "Not at all likely" and 10 being "Extremely likely"
Target	+75

Learner Intention to Apply Learning

Level 1 evaluation instruments that measure learners' intentions for applying what they learned during a training program on the job provide insights into learners' perceived utility of the initiative. Level 1 items that measure intention may include these questions:

- How likely are you to apply what you have learned in this training to your job? (Use a five-point scale, with 5 being *very likely* and 1 being *very unlikely*.)
- How likely are you to use [*insert specific skill taught during the course*] within the next 90 days? (Use a five-point scale, with 5 being *very likely* and 1 being *very unlikely*.)
- I intend to use [*insert specific skill taught during the course*] on the job. (Use a five-point scale, with 5 being *very likely* and 1 being *very unlikely*.)
- What are three things you plan to do differently as a result of completing this training program? (Open-ended item)
- What is one thing from this training program that you plan to implement in the next 90 days? (Open-ended item)

Learner Perception of Learning

Table B-3 provides examples of Level 1 items that measure perceptions of learning as part of a Level 1 instrument.

Table B-3. Level 1 Items

#	Item	Prior to Attending	After Attending
		5 = Exceptional 1 = Poor	
1.	How would you rate your ability to identify coniferous trees?		
2.	How would you rate your ability to differentiate between coniferous trees and deciduous trees?		

Level 2: Learning

Level 2 instruments measure learning—acquisition of new knowledge, skills, and attitudes—that occurred because of learner participation in the initiative. They should be designed with items that prove learners are able to demonstrate proficiency in the course's learning objectives. Each item should connect (directly or indirectly) to one or more of the established learning objectives for the course. If not, either the item shouldn't be on the instrument, or a learning objective may be missing.

Level 2 items may be closed-ended or open-ended. Higher-order open-ended items that ask learners to explain a given topic require learners to demonstrate their comprehension of the information. Observations, role plays, and simulations are examples of Level 2 evaluation activities that measure learning at the cognitive (information and mental procedures), affective, and psychomotor (psychomotor procedures) domains. These types of Level 2 activities themselves are not instruments. Rather, the rubrics used by an evaluator (such as an instructor, facilitator, observer, or peer reviewer) to assess learners' performance against established criteria are the Level 2 evaluation instruments, and the individual observable behaviors are the Level 2 instrument items.

For example, a course on trees has the following learning objectives:
- Given a list of trees (condition), learners will be able to identify the names of coniferous trees (performance) with 100 percent accuracy (criterion).
- Without the use of any sources (condition), learners will be able to differentiate between a coniferous tree and a deciduous tree (performance) with 100 percent accuracy (criterion).

Table B-4 presents possible corresponding Level 2 instrument items to measure learning.

Table B-4. Possible Level 2 Instrument Items

Level 2 Instrument Items	Item Linked to Objectives

A. Identify which trees in this list are coniferous:
  ◦ Maple   ◦ White pine   ◦ Oak
  ◦ Walnut   ◦ Blue spruce   ◦ Juniper
	1

B. True or False? All coniferous trees produce cones.	2
C. Describe the differences between a coniferous tree and a deciduous tree.	2
D. True of False? Trees are sentient.	None

Items that aren't directly or indirectly aligned with one or more learning objectives shouldn't be included in a Level 2 instrument. In Table B-4, no learning objective was related to item D—whether trees are sentient (have the ability to perceive or feel). In addition, that isn't a distinguishing quality between coniferous and deciduous trees. Therefore, it shouldn't be included. If learners needed to acquire knowledge about sentient beings, this should have been an explicit (direct) or implied (indirect) learning objective. Item B is an example of a Level 2 instrument item that has an implied alignment with learning objective 2. Although that learning objective doesn't explicitly state anything about trees producing cones, cone-bearing is the distinguishing quality that differentiates coniferous and deciduous trees, so learners must possess that knowledge to demonstrate proficiency in the learning objective. Therefore, the item is appropriate because it measures learners' knowledge related to learning objective 2.

Knowledge checks, quizzes, tests, and exams are among the most popular Level 2 instruments. They can be the easiest and cheapest to create and administer. These Level 2 instruments can only measure learning in the cognitive domain. However, it's impossible for them to measure learning in the psychomotor domain, because doing so requires learners to demonstrate observable behaviors.

While Level 2 items may be closed-ended or open-ended, closed-ended items require learners to, at minimum, recall information they learned. Multiple-choice, select-all-that-apply, true or false, and matching are examples of closed-ended items, because they contain the information necessary to correctly answer each one. Open-ended items on Level 2 instruments must also have a correct answer and should not collect reactions, opinions, intentions, or perceptions.

Table B-5 includes some examples of Level 2 items.

Table B-5. Examples of Level 2 Items

Level 2 Item That Measures Knowledge or Information	Level 2 Item That Measures Comprehension or Mental Procedures

Which of the following is an example of a coniferous tree?
  A. Maple
  B. White pine
  C. Oak
  D. Walnut
	Correctly identify the order of operations to calculate this equation: $a + (b - x) \div y$
	  A. Subtract x from b. Divide by y. Add a.
	  B. Add a and b. Subtract x. Divide by y.
	  C. Divide x by y. Subtract from b. Add a.
	  D. Subtract x from b. Add a. Divide by y.

(B) is the correct answer	(A) is the correct answer
If the course material included a chart that listed coniferous trees and deciduous trees, a learner may have memorized the chart and recalled that a white pine is a coniferous tree. However, answering this item correctly doesn't prove that a learner knows the difference between a coniferous and deciduous tree—or even the definition of a coniferous tree, which would be a higher-order item that measures comprehension.	The learner would have to know the order of operations, which requires more than simply recalling information. It requires understanding and comprehension. A correct answer doesn't indicate whether the learner can actually calculate the answer using a formula with numbers rather than variables. Rather, a correct answer—unless it's a lucky guess—indicates only that a student comprehends the process for calculating the equation.
Level 2 Item That Measures Application or Mental Procedures	**Level 2 Item That Measures Comprehension or Mental Procedures**
A pizza chef uses a dough recipe that calls for 1,000 grams of tipo "00" flour, 600 milliliters of water, 10 grams of active yeast, and 25 grams of salt. The recipe makes six batches of dough of about 172 grams each. Each pizza is about 12 inches wide and feeds one to two people. The chef only has 700 grams of tipo "00" flour and needs to adjust the recipe using baker's percentages.	Describe the steps necessary to fly a plane from starting the engines to takeoff. Be sure to identify and explain the order in which levels, dials, and controls are used, and explain what each does.

How many milliliters of water will the recipe require if the chef uses 700 grams of flour?
  A. 600 ml
  B. 428 ml
  C. 420 ml
  D. 500 ml
	[Insert short answer.]

Table B-5. (cont.)

Level 2 Item That Measures Application or Mental Procedures	Level 2 Item That Measures Comprehension or Mental Procedures
(C) is the correct answer	The assessor will have to determine the quality and accuracy of the response. Answers may range from completely incorrect to 100% correct.
There are two ways a learner could answer this item correctly: a lucky guess, or understanding how baker's percentages work and applying their knowledge by calculating the correct amount of water needed to adjust the recipe based on the amount of flour.	This item measures a learner's ability to describe how a plane is flown but doesn't measure whether they're actually able to fly a plane. Hence, this is a cognitive or knowledge item rather than a psychomotor item.

There are several ways to use Level 2 instruments to assess skill proficiency. Use **dichotomous instruments** to evaluate if a skill was observed. Either the learner was observed performing the skill (correctly or incorrectly) or wasn't observed performing the skill at all. An example of a Level 2 instrument intended to assess a learner's ability to demonstrate learning at the psychomotor skill level would be a rubric used by a driver's education instructor to assess a new driver's ability to start a car correctly (Table B-6).

Table B-6. Example of a Dichotomous Level 2 Instrument

#	Behavior	Observed		Not Observed
		Correct	Incorrect	
1	Adjusted seat			x
2	Adjusted mirrors	x		
3	Pressed foot on brake petal		x	
4	Placed key in ignition	x		
5	Turned key clockwise to engage engine		x	

Degree of proficiency instruments rely upon behaviorally anchored rating scales (BARS) to determine the degree to which a learner accurately performs a skill. An example of a Level 2 instrument intended to assess the degree to which a learner demonstrated learning in the psychomotor domain would be a rubric used by an instructor to assess the degree of proficiency of a learner's public-speaking skills (Table B-7).

Table B-7. Example of a Degree of Proficiency Instrument

#	Behavior	Performance Rating Scale				
		Excellent	Exceeds Expectations	Meets Expectations	Falls Below Expectations	Unacceptable
		5	4	3	2	1
1	Eye contact	Excellent use of eye contact; majority of time is spent making eye contact with audience	Very good use of eye contact; spent more time making eye contact than looking at notes or the screen	Good use of eye contact; spent more time looking at the audience than notes or the screen	Fair use of eye contact; spent more time looking at notes or the screen than the audience	Unacceptable eye contact; spent most of the time looking at notes or the screen rather than the audience; avoided eye contact
2	Volume	Excellent with volume; used inflections in volume and tone appropriately to emphasize points and gain audience attention	Very good with volume; very consistent with projection; very audible; very clear enunciation	Good with volume; mostly consistent in projection; audible; mostly clear enunciation	Fair with volume; somewhat consistent in projection; difficult to hear at times; difficult to understand at times	Unacceptable with volume; very difficult to hear; very difficult to understand
3	Organization	Excellent with content organization; content was masterfully delivered in a logical and compelling way that resonated with the audience	Very good with content organization; content structured in coherent, meaningful way	Good with content organization; presentation flowed relatively smoothly	Fair with content organization; presentation seemed disjointed; flow of information needed work	Unacceptable with content organization; presentation was disjointed; content was disorganized
4	...	...	...	...	...	...

Level 3: Behavior or Application

Level 3 instruments are often the same instruments used in Level 2 evaluations measuring changes in learners' observable behaviors. For example, an observation instrument can be used during a training course (Level 2) and then subsequently on the job (Level 3). On the job, the instrument may be administered by supervisors, managers, learners (self-assessments), direct reports, colleagues, or customers. Collecting the same data from several different evaluators is considered "investigator triangulation" and can be important for establishing data validity and reliability (Russ-Eft and Preskill 2009).

As part of measuring behavior change, Level 3 instruments may include both closed-ended and open-ended items. Closed-ended items may include self-assessments from learners regarding the frequency of behavior change on the job and management support. These aren't reactions but measures of the cadence of actual behavior change. Open-ended Level 3 items allow learners to describe and explain how they are (or aren't) applying what they learned in the course to their jobs. They might include the examples in Table B-8.

Table B-8. Level 3 Instrument Examples

#	Item	
1.	How often do you [*insert skill taught in course*]?	5—Always 4—Often 3—Sometimes 2—Rarely 1—Never
2.	How often does your direct supervisor or manager encourage you to [*insert skill taught in course*]?	5—Always 4—Often 3—Sometimes 2—Rarely 1—Never
3	Describe how you apply what you learned during the course to your job.	Open-ended
4.	What challenges do you experience while applying what you learned in the course to your job?	Open-ended

Remember, Level 1 evaluations measure reactions, and Level 3 evaluations measure behaviors and application on the job. While most Level 1 evaluations are conducted at the end of or immediately following a course, they can also be conducted at the same time as Level 3 evaluations. Doing so can prove useful in measuring learners' reactions to conditions on the job (rather than during the course) that encourage or discourage training transfer. Table B-9 shows Level 1 instrument items that you might include alongside Level 3.

Table B-9. Level 1 Instruments Used With Level 3 Instruments

#	Item	
1.	My direct supervisor or manager encourages me to apply what I learned during training to my job.	5—Strongly agree 4—Agree 3—Neutral 2—Disagree 1—Strongly disagree
2.	Applying what I learned during the course has improved my performance.	5—Strongly agree 4—Agree 3—Neutral 2—Disagree 1—Strongly disagree
3	Describe how your supervisor or manager encourages or discourages you to apply what you learned during the training program to your job.	Open-ended

Training transfer requires a strong partnership between talent development professionals and business leaders. If the application environment (or the environment where the job is performed after training) isn't conducive to transfer, or if management isn't supportive of employees using the knowledge, skills, and attitudes they learned during the training program while on the job, it can compromise the overall success and negate any contributions of talent development. To ensure success on the job, there are several ways you can promote transfer:

- **Ensure that learning environments mimic application environments as much as possible.** To the extent the two environments are similar, training transfer may be easier for learners and more likely to occur. If they're dissimilar, the application environment may impede transfer.
- **Consider learners' attitudes about behavior changes—how they think and feel about such changes (affective domain).**

Gaining their buy-in so they're adopters rather than compliers can go a long way in supporting transfer.

- **Ensure supervisors and managers understand the importance of monitoring behaviors on the job** and are making every effort to encourage and reinforce the behaviors on the job.
- **Collaborate with business leaders to incentivize training transfer.** This might include updating or upgrading tools and equipment, introducing compensation programs that reward learners for transferring behaviors, and creating conditions on the job that promote transfer (such as signage that reminds and encourages workers to apply what they learned).
- **Business leaders should hold learners and their supervisors and managers accountable for ensuring transfer occurs on the job.** This should be reflected in performance discussions or documentation and used as the basis of administrative decisions around pay, promotion, and further involvement in TD initiatives (such as mentoring and training).

Level 4: Results or Impact

To correlate business results with the outcomes of TD initiatives, it's important to isolate the effects of training. Remember, as you collaborate with business leaders on the percent of a business goal you agree training can achieve, you identify several strategies beyond training that can contribute meaningfully to producing results. To determine the extent that training contributed, you might use control groups, conduct trend analyses, and perform estimations.

Using Control Groups

The use of control groups is the most credible technique when the experiment is well designed. They're helpful for demonstrating the difference in performance of a measure, comparing that of a trained group (treatment group) with that of an untrained group (control group). To ensure validity and reliability of the outcome, members of each group should be selected randomly (if possible), and the groups should be structured in a way that provides a meaningful comparison in terms of size, sales market, product and service mix, management, and incentive pay programs. For example, at the end of the experiment, the overall sales performance of the treatment group is compared with the overall sales performance of the control group. If the overall sales performance of the treatment group was $2 million, and the overall sales performance of the control group was $1.5 million, the benefit that may be attributed to training is calculated as follows: benefit = $2 million – $1.5 million = $500,000.

The benefit is $500,000 rather than $2 million (the overall sales performance of the treatment group) because the control group sold $1.5 million without undergoing any training. It is a reasonable assumption that if the treatment group hadn't undergone training, it would have experienced the same overall sales performance. Only the difference between the two groups can be considered the benefit of training.

Conducting Trend Analyses

You can use this technique in detecting changes in performance or business results over a period of time to consider what events may have affected fluctuations in results. For example, a sales team tracks sales weekly. Given a five-year history, variability in sales has been consistent year-over-year. Once the company put its sales team through sales training in August of a given year, it detected a noticeable increase in sales the following September, well above the average sales for the past five Septembers, each $1.5 million. The September immediately following sales training reported sales of $2 million, an increase of $500,000. Given no other extraneous variables, the company could reasonably attribute the increase in sales to the sales training, which would be further reinforced by feedback received from salespeople, supervisors, managers, subordinates, colleagues, and customers. Therefore, the benefit of the sales training program would be about $500,000.

For this approach to work, however, four conditions must be met:

- The data must exist; that is, it must come from a system and be data that the organization tracks routinely.
- The data must be stable so the trend is consistent for a period of time that is meaningful to a particular measure.
- The trend would likely continue if nothing else happens.
- No other factors that could influence the measure occurred during the evaluation period.

Performing Estimations

Calculating estimations of training benefits is another approach to isolating the effects of training, particularly when control groups and trend analyses aren't practical or available. For example, a sales organization wants to know how much an improvement in sales is due to the sales training. If a control group and trend-line analysis is not feasible, it may fall back on the estimation process. The first step is to determine the improvement in sales. Next, identify the most credible source of information for how much of the improvement is due to the program. Sometimes the most credible source is the learner; sometimes it's the supervisor; sometimes it's multiple sources, including those stakeholders who identified efforts to address the sales problem in the first place. Then, ask your source these questions:

- What caused improvement in the measure?
- How much of the improvement is due to sales training?
- How confident are you in your estimate?

The result of the process will be the most conservative estimate of how much the increase in the measure is due to the program. This is your Level 4 impact.

For instance, say there was an increase in sales of $2.1 million. You decide that you will conduct a focus group of the sales team, which includes participants in the sales training program, along with their managers. You share the fact that there has been an increase in sales and then ask them what caused it. Because other factors were identified during the analysis, you might start the conversation with this list. In addition to this list, the group may identify other factors that they believe influenced sales. Then you ask them to estimate as a percentage how much of the increase in sales is due to each factor. To ensure the most conservative estimate, you ask them to indicate, as a percentage, how confident they are in their estimates. Remember, these people don't have a stake in the results and have no reason to overstate or understate their estimates.

Table B-10 shows how the process plays out. A variety of initiatives (column A) have been identified that likely led to this increase. As part of step 3 of the eight-step Evaluation-Focused Instructional Design Framework, business leaders agreed on an initial estimate of the percentage for each initiative in column A. At the conclusion of the initiative, an average estimate of how much of the improvement was due to each factor is then calculated (column C). Note that this column should always equal 100 percent. Then, the average confidence in the estimate of how much each factor contributed to the improvement is calculated (column D). Multiplying column C by column D results in the adjusted contribution of each factor (column E). This column tells you how much of the improvement in sales is due to each factor. If you're interested in how much of the improvement in sales is due to the sales training, the answer would be 13.5 percent of $2.1 million, or $283,500 in sales.

Table B-10. Estimations Process

Business Goal	Increase US sales by $2.5 million by December 31, 2024			
Actual Results	US sales increased by $2.1 million by December 31, 2024			
Initiative (A)	Initial Estimate From Step 4 (B)	Avg Estimated Contribution (C)	% Confidence (D)	Adj % (E) C x D = E
New products	20%	30%	90%	27%
Pricing adjustments	10%	5%	85%	4.25%
Marketing initiatives	20%	15%	75%	11.25%
Increase sales force	15%	25%	95%	23.75%
Incentive pay program	15%	10%	95%	9.5%
Sales training	20%	15%	90%	13.5%
	100%	100%		

Level 5: Return on Investment (ROI)

Level 5 evaluations measure the results of TD initiatives using the language of business—money. Unlike all other levels of evaluation, Level 5 uses a formula:

$$ROI = \frac{Benefits - Costs}{Costs} \times 100$$

Although the formula alone may give the impression that such a calculation is easy to perform, calculating the monetary value of benefits and costs requires work. Ideally, you complete this work in the analysis phase, during problem identification and quantification, as well as by pricing out the solution to the problem. At that point, it becomes a math problem.

Results of the Level 4 evaluation represent the impact to the business due to the program. To prepare for the ROI formula, convert the impact measures to money using the same technique used during the analysis phase:

- Standard values can be used for sales, productivity, and time.
  » The standard value for a sale is the gross profit on the sale.
  » For productivity, it's the standard set by the organization.
  » For time, it's the cost of a person's time based on their salary plus benefits.
- Historical costs can be used for measures that don't have a standard value but have an available receipt or record.
- Expert input can be used for measures without a standard value or record, but that have an expert in the area with enough knowledge to provide the monetary benefit.
- Databases can offer credible research describing the monetary value of a measure. You might use EBSCOhost, ERIC, and Google Scholar, but other research organizations may also provide insight into the monetary values of measures that matter.
- Statistical analysis connects softer measures to measures more easily converted to money.
- Estimations can be used when there are no other options and knowing the monetary value for the measure is important.

Calculating the fully loaded cost of a program is important, particularly when reporting the ROI. Implementing a solution costs the organization much more than hiring a consultant, purchasing a program, or even developing a program. You need to determine the amount that was required to analyze, design, develop, and implement a training program, including hard costs (expenses related to licensing materials, printing, or hiring an instructor) and soft costs (salaries of TD professionals, wages of learners while participating in training, and costs associated with lost productivity).

The fully loaded costs also include the cost of the evaluation. While some people would argue that the evaluation cost category is one reason they don't pursue Level 4 and Level 5 evaluations, an ROI study should cost you no more than 5 to 10 percent of the total program costs. That represents pennies when you consider the value of the information coming from such an evaluation.

But remember, this type of analysis is not necessary for all training initiatives. Evaluation at Levels 4 and 5 is usually reserved for expensive, strategic, and operationally aligned programs—and ones that stakeholders have a keen interest in knowing the value of the money they're spending on a program.

Here is a simple example of how the ROI calculation works. A company increased sales for one year by $378,000, and you know that the increase is due to the program because you isolated the effects of the program using a control group. While sales are already measured in money, it's important to convert them to profit using the gross profit margin to appropriately report the value of increasing sales to the company. In this case the profit margin is 10 percent, so the monetary benefit of the increase in sales is $37,800. The fully loaded cost of the sales training program is $25,000. Therefore, the ROI is:

$$ROI = \frac{\text{Benefits} - \text{Costs}}{\text{Costs}} \times 100$$

$$ROI = \frac{\$37{,}800 - \$25{,}000}{\$25{,}000} \times 100$$

$$ROI = \frac{\$12{,}800}{\$25{,}000} \times 100 = 51.2\%$$

An ROI of 51.2 percent tells stakeholders that for every $1 they invest in the sales training program, they'll receive that dollar back plus an additional $51.20 over and beyond the $1 investment. When comparing this return with that of typical investments, this is a great ROI.

What makes a good ROI? Some people suggest that an ROI of 100 percent is necessary for a TD initiative to be successful. That is far from the truth. In fact, programs with that type of return are rare. High ROIs often occur when organizations invest in leadership development, executive coaching, and supervisor training. When the right people are involved in these programs at the right time and they target measures under their control and that their teams can influence, then it's possible to see substantial returns. High ROIs also occur when there is an expensive problem that can be solved by an inexpensive solution, and the solution works. But again, these aren't common.

A good ROI depends on the target, which is typically set using one of four techniques (Phillips and Phillips 2015):

- **Using break-even as the target.** This is a 0 percent ROI. Break-even indicates the program paid for itself, although there is no additional gain. Many ROI targets set at break-even are found when evaluating programs delivered to nonprofits, governments, and nongovernmental organizations. Although, for some programs, even these organizations want a benefit that exceeds costs.
- **Setting the ROI target at the same level of return as other investments made by the organization.** Depending on what investments the organization is making, this could range between 10 and 18 percent. The benefit of using this as your target is that it aligns with other returns.
- **Setting the target at 25 percent.** This ROI objective is most typical primarily because over time, we have seen investments pay off at the 25 percent target or more. It's also a good indicator to stakeholders that by investing in the development of people, the organization can reap the same benefit as when it invests in other ways, if not a greater benefit.
- **Partnering with the client to set the target.** This is the ideal approach. And, if you follow the process described in this book, you will set the ROI target before you ever design the program. Working with the client to set the ROI is beneficial because it opens the door to a conversation about their role in making the program successful.

Given access to enough historical data, a target can also be set based on mathematical models. Regardless of how the target is set, it's important to remember that an ROI (and any other level of results) is only as good as what it is compared with. ROI can vary for many reasons, so comparing the ROI of a program with its target or with the ROI of another program in isolation of other measures and context is insufficient. You must report the full story of program success, which includes results at the lower levels of evaluation.

Appendix C
General Guidelines for Evaluation

An important competency for TD practitioners who use the eight-step Evaluation-Focused Instructional Design Framework proposed in this book is the ability to design and develop effective evaluation instruments composed of appropriate evaluation items. The following guidelines offer best practices for creating sound evaluation instruments so that you can adequately and accurately measure reactions, learning, behavior or application, results or impact, and ROI.

Instruments are sets of items used to collect data. *Items* are the individual questions or statements that elicit data from responders. For example, a survey administered at the end of a course (Level 1) is an instrument; each question or statement that appears as part of the survey is an item.

Instrument items collect two types of data. *Key evaluation data* provides insights into how learners think, what they know, how they feel, what they can do, what they intend to do, and what they have done. *Demographic data* simply provides contextual information about the responder (age, race, or gender) and allows for slicing and dicing data by various characteristics. Some best practices will ensure your data is high quality and tells you what you need to know.

Key Evaluation Data Can Be Collected in Two Ways
Whether you construct instrument items as open-ended or closed-ended will influence how a learner may respond.

Closed-Ended Items

Closed-ended items are qualitative data points measured using only the options provided as viable responses. Such responses could be as simple as a "yes" or "no," or as sophisticated as a ranked order among several response choices. Closed-ended items don't provide an opportunity for responders to deviate from predetermined options. One of their benefits is you can easily measure and quantify them. For example, for an item measuring strength of agreement, it would be easy to find a percent-favorable score by determining the number of respondents who answered "4" and "5" and dividing by the total number of respondents. Likewise, you can easily calculate a percent-unfavorable score by determining the number of respondents who answered "1" and "2" and dividing by the total number of respondents. You can ascertain a percent-neutral score by determining the number of respondents who answered "3" and dividing by the total number of respondents. Table C-1 illustrates an example.

Table C-1. Closed-Ended Items

Item: I intend to apply what I learned in this course to my job.

#	Anchor	# Respondents				Quantitative Data
5	Strongly Agree	42	56.8%	69	69/74	93.2% Favorable
4	Agree	27	36.5%			
3	Neutral	4	5.4%	4	4/74	5.4% Neutral
2	Disagree	1	1.4%	1	1/74	1.4% Unfavorable
1	Strongly Disagree	0	0.0%			
		74	100%	74	74/74	100%

The reason you want to report percent-favorable, percent-neutral, and percent-unfavorable rather than reporting data for all five anchors is that you're trying to understand overall reactions of learners—did they respond favorably, neutrally, or unfavorably? And because each responder may have different criteria for distinguishing between what qualifies as "strongly agree" and "agree," it's helpful to know what percentage of respondents answered favorably overall. It's helpful to know the data for each anchor as well because you may want to measure how many learners you can move from responding with a 4 to responding with a 5, and how many learners you can move from responding with a 3 to responding with a 4, for example.

Open-Ended Items

Open-ended items are generally qualitative and allow respondents to answer any way they wish. In surveys, open-ended items are constructed with text fields that allow for writing or typing a response. An example of an open-ended item is asking learners to share one thing they'll apply within the next 90 days after completing a course. Each respondent may answer differently. To determine if there is a pattern or trend among qualitative, open-ended data, you must code the responses during your data analysis. For example, in response to the question, "What is one thing you learned during this course that you will apply within the next 90 days?" you might receive these answers:

- "Active listening skills" (listening)
- "Listening for customer needs" (listening)
- "Understanding what customers want" (listening)
- "Asking clarifying questions" (asking questions)
- "Repeating back what I heard to verify my understanding" (checking for understanding)
- "Asking questions to demonstrate listening" (asking questions)
- "Ask more questions" (asking questions)

These responses can be coded in multiple ways. For example, they might all be coded as "actively listening" because they're all behaviors that would be expected as part of active listening. Or they might be coded in a way that further clarifies exactly what behaviors of actively listening the respondents intend to apply; for example, in this list three responses (42.9 percent) were about listening, three responses (42.9 percent) were about asking questions, and one (14.3 percent) response was about checking for understanding.

Consider the Appropriate Rating Scale for Closed-Ended Items

Many closed-ended items use a Likert scale with several ratings responders can choose from. Originally proposed by American psychologist Rensis Likert in 1932 as part of a PhD dissertation to measure people's feelings and attitudes relative to international affairs, the Likert scale is commonly used in social research and for conducting evaluations. In the TD profession, the Likert scale is frequently used to measure Level 1 learner reactions. It was originally a strength of agreement scale, whereby respondents would be asked to respond to a question or statement and indicate their strength of agreement (Figure C-1).

Figure C-1. Strength of Agreement Scale

Strongly Agree	Agree	Neutral	Disagree	Strongly Disagree
5	4	3	2	1

Since the Likert scale's initial introduction, several adaptations have been introduced to measure different feelings and attitudes on the five-point scale, with 5 being the most favorable, and 1 being the least favorable (Figure C-2).

Figure C-2. Likert Scale Adaptations

	5	4	3	2	1
Strength of satisfaction	Very satisfied	Satisfied	Neutral	Unsatisfied	Very unsatisfied
Strength of likelihood	Very likely	Likely	Unsure	Unlikely	Very unlikely
Degree of quality	Excellent	Very good	Good	Fair	Poor
Degree of favorability	Very favorable	Favorable	Neutral	Unfavorable	Very unfavorable
Frequency	Always	Often	Sometimes	Rarely	Never
Frequency	Very frequently	Frequently	Occasionally	Infrequently	Very infrequently
Strength of preference	Very desirable	Desirable	Neutral	Undesirable	Very undesirable
Degree of appropriateness	Very appropriate	Appropriate	Neutral	Inappropriate	Very inappropriate
Degree of applicability	Very applicable	Applicable	Neutral	Unapplicable	Very unapplicable
Degree of importance	Very important	Important	Neutral	Unimportant	Very unimportant
Degree of priority	Essential	High priority	Medium priority	Low priority	Not a priority
Performance (behaviorally anchored rating scale, or BARS)	Exceptional	Exceeds expectations	Fully meets expectations	Falls below expectations	Unacceptable

In addition to selecting an appropriate scale for closed-ended items, it is important to also consider the order in which ratings appear. For responders in the United States, there may be an unconscious tendency to assume a higher number is a more favorable response. For example, a score of 5 will generally be "Exceeds Expectations," "Strongly Agree," or "Very Likely," whereas a score of 1 will generally be "Unacceptable, "Strongly Disagree," or "Very Unlikely." If you were to invert the numerical rating scale, with 1 being favorable and 5 being unfavorable, respondents may not notice and instinctively respond using the rating structure they are most familiar with rather than the one you've provided.

Be Consistent With the Use of Scales

It can be very confusing for learners when the scale changes for each item. For example, if you use a strength of agreement scale, try to use only a strength of agreement scale for all non-open-ended items. If you absolutely need to change scales to collect additional data other than agreement (perhaps likelihood), be sure to construct the instrument in a way that makes it very clear that there is a change in scale. If you need to switch scales on items, alert the respondent that the scale is changing. And, of course, be sure that the scale makes sense for the item. If possible, group like scales together so they do not change from item to item.

Be Brief

Brevity is especially critical when using Level 1 survey instruments. At the end of a course, learners will probably not want to spend a lot of time completing surveys. If they see the survey is fairly quick to complete, they may be more inclined to do so. I prefer to keep Level 1 survey instruments to no more than 10 items, which requires me to prioritize which 10 pieces of data will be most helpful when evaluating the success of an initiative.

Collect Only Data You Will Use

Only include items on the instrument that elicit data you will actually use in some meaningful way, or else you may deter respondents. My mantra is: "If you aren't going to use it, don't ask for it." Whenever I see Level 1 survey instruments that ask for learners' names, I always wonder how that data will be used. It should only be collected if it *will* be used. Soliciting demographic data like learners' names may deter responses. I collect mostly key data rather than demographic data.

My mantra is: "If you aren't going to use it, don't ask for it."

Avoid Collecting Unnecessary Demographic Information

Unless you plan to analyze data by segmenting learner audiences by demographic, there is very little need to collect demographic data. If, however, you want to be able to analyze how responses of learners 20 to 29 years old compare with those of learners 40 to 49 years old, you might need to ask for this data point. However, don't ask *just in case* you might be interested at some point in time. Ask only if you know up front that you want to perform that level of analysis.

Leave Demographic Items for the End

If you find you do want to analyze data by segmenting learners by demographic, you should leave demographic items for the end of the survey. While those data points might be important for your analysis, they're useless if learners don't respond to the key items that provide the information you want to analyze. If learners start to complete a survey and then experience fatigue, they may simply stop responding. It's better to collect the key data without demographic data than it is to collect demographic data without key data.

Avoid Item Construction Errors

You need to carefully construct each item on an evaluation instrument. Avoid these common errors:

- **Leading items**—items that may appear to lead the respondent to answer a particular way. For example, asking learners to indicate how much they loved a course presumes that they loved the course. Instead, you might ask, "On a scale of 1 to 5, how did you find the course? 5 = Extremely Helpful, 4 = Helpful, 3 = Neutral, 2 = Unhelpful, 1 = Extremely Unhelpful."

- **Loaded items**—avoid using loaded items that trick people into a favorable response. For example, don't say, "I will recommend this awesome course to others." Even if a respondent answers negatively, the item is measuring the likelihood of their referral, so a negative response does not indicate disagreement that the course was awesome. By simply answering the loaded item, the respondent is tricked into essentially agreeing that the course was awesome. So, even if 74 out of 74 learners responded to the item with an unfavorable rating, the data could be misrepresented as though 100 percent of learners indicated the course was awesome, even though 0 percent indicated they would refer anyone else. Avoid loaded items by refraining from using positive (or negative) adjectives.
- **Compound items**—avoid using compound items that ask two separate things (also known as double-barreled items). For example, don't say, "The instructor was knowledgeable and encouraged learner interaction." The issue here is the item is attempting to measure two variables: the instructor's knowledge and the instructor's efforts to encourage learner interaction. These two variables are not mutually exclusive; while they both could be true, one can be true without the other being true. And a respondent might agree with one of them and disagree with the other. How are they supposed to answer if the instructor was very knowledgeable but made no effort to encourage learner interaction? If the learner answers the item affirmatively, you must assume both are true. If the learner answers the item negatively, you must assume both are false. Avoid eliciting two data points (such as instructor knowledge and encouragement of interaction) in the same item. If an evaluation instrument contains the word and, it's likely a compound item. If both data points are important in understanding what success looks like from a Level 1 perspective, elicit the data using two discrete items.
- **Absolutes**—avoid using absolutes in items such as "always" and "never." For example, don't say, "One a scale of 1 to 5, indicate your strength of agreement with the following statement: I always take notes when I attend courses. (5 = Strongly Agree, 4 = Agree,

3 = Neutral, 2 = Disagree, 1 = Strongly Disagree)." The issue with absolute statements like this is that if it is false one time in a billion, the learner cannot agree with it and is therefore essentially forced to respond with at least a 2. If you avoid an absolute by swapping "always" with "often" or "usually," the learner could respond with a 4 or 5.

- **Double negative items**—be careful to avoid double negatives in items. For example, don't say, "I do not think this course should not be mandatory." If a respondent answers favorably, they are answering that they think the course should be mandatory.

- **Dichotomous items**—avoid items that can be answered one way or another, such as "yes" or "no." It may be more useful to reframe dichotomous questions so a respondent can indicate a strength of agreement. For example, the item "I am knowledgeable about the features of [*insert product name*]" is dichotomous and can be answered with a simple yes or no response. Consider reframing the item like this: "How would you rate your knowledge of the features of [*insert product name*]?" And use a strength of quality scale: 5 = Excellent, 4 = Very Good, 3 = Good, 2 = Fair, 1 = Poor. This can help you understand the degree of knowledge learners self-perceive and indicate if more work might be required to improve knowledge of product features.

Look for Patterns and Trends

Especially with open-ended comments, try to piece together responses that show trends. If many responders answer similarly, it establishes that the response isn't isolated or an outlier. If the pattern or trend is positive, it indicates a generally favorable reaction to the initiative. If the pattern or trend is negative, it indicates an opportunity to follow up with learners to provide any additional information or support they may need and make improvements to the initiative before it's offered again. Try not to get distracted by negative responses.

Consider When and How to Administer Evaluations

When and how you administer evaluation instruments may have an impact on the number of respondents who participate. For example, if you administer a hard copy reaction survey at the end of a course before learners are dismissed, you might get a higher response rate than if you administered an electronic survey a day or more after the course.

References

Anderson, L.W., D.R. Krathwohl, P.W. Airasian, K.A. Cruikshank, R.E. Mayer, P.R. Pintrich, J. Raths, and M.C. Wittrock, eds. 2001. *A Taxonomy for Learning, Teaching, and Assessing: A Revision of Bloom's Taxonomy of Educational Objectives.* New York: Longman.

ASQ (American Society for Quality). n.d. "What Are Stakeholders?" ASQ, Quality Resources. asq.org/quality-resources/stakeholders.

Association for Talent Development (ATD). n.d. "About Us." td.org/about.

Burton, J.K., and P.F. Merrill. 1991. "Needs Assessment: Goals, Needs and Priorities." In *Instructional Design Principles and Applications*, edited by L.J. Briggs, K.L. Gustafson, and M.H. Tillman, 17–43. Englewood Cliffs, NJ: Educational Technology Publications.

Confino, P. 2022. "Here Are the 20 Biggest Automakers in the World." *Fortune*, August 12. fortune.com/2022/08/12/20-biggest-car-companies-world-fortune-global-500.

Dave, R.H. 1975. *Developing and Writing Behavioral Objectives*, edited by R.J. Armstrong. Tucson, AZ: Educational Innovators Press.

Feeding America. n.d. "About Feeding America." feedingamerica.org/about-us.

Gagné, R.M., L.J. Briggs, and W.W. Wager, eds. 1992. *Principles of Instructional Design.* Fort Worth, TX: Harcourt Brace Jovanovich.

IACET (International Accreditors for Continuing Education and Training). n.d. "Home—IACET." iacet.org.

Ingraham, C. 2017. "What's a Urinal Fly, and What Does It Have to Do With Winning a Nobel Prize?" *Washington Post,* October 9. washingtonpost .com/news/wonk/wp/2017/10/09/whats-a-urinal-fly-and-what-does -it-have-to-with-winning-a-nobel-prize.

Krathwohl, D.R., B.S. Bloom, and B.B. Masia. 1964. *Taxonomy of Educational Objectives, the Classification of Educational Goals. Handbook II: Affective Domain.* New York: David McKay Co.

Likert, R. 1932. "A Technique for the Measurement of Attitudes." *Archives of Psychology*: 1–55.

Mager, R.F. 1997. *Preparing Instructional Objectives: A Critical Tool in the Development of Effective Instruction,* 3rd ed. Atlanta: The Center for Effective Performance.

Ohno, T. 1988. *Toyota Production System: Beyond Large-Scale Production.* Portland, OR: Productivity Press.

Phillips, P.P., and J.J. Phillips. 2015. *Real World Training Evaluation.* Alexandria, VA: ATD Press.

Reichheld, F. 2011. *The Ultimate Question 2.0: How Net Promoter Companies Thrive in a Customer-Driven World.* Boston: Harvard Business Press.

Russ-Eft, D.F., and H. Preskill. 2009. *Evaluation in Organizations: A Systematic Approach to Enhancing Learning, Performance, and Change.* New York: Basic Books.

Samsung. n.d. "Leadership & Mission | About Us." samsung.com/us/about -us/leadership-and-mission.

Sawhill, J., and D. Williamson. 2001. "Measuring What Matters in Nonprofits." McKinsey and Company, May 1. mckinsey.com/industries/public-and -social-sector/our-insights/measuring-what-matters-in-nonprofits.

Moloney, C. 2022. "10 Employee Onboarding Statistics you Must Know in 2022." Kallidus. kallidus.com/resources/blog/10-employee-onboarding -statistics-you-must-know-in-2022.

United. n.d. "Diversity, Equity, and Inclusion | United Airlines." united.com /ual/en/us/fly/company/global-citizenship/diversity.html.

US Air Force. 1993. *Instructional System Development.* AFM 36-2234. Washington, DC: U.S. Government Printing Office.

Index

Note: Page numbers followed by *f* or *t* indicate figures or tables.

A

absolutes, avoiding in evaluation instruments, 175–176

achievable business goals, business challenges and, 104–105, 105*t*

actualized versus aspirational culture, 39–43, 40*t*, 47

ADDIE (analysis, design, development, implementation, and evaluation), reimagined, 14–17

    evaluation of success of, 122–123, 123*t*, 124*t*, 126*f*, 127*f*

adopter stakeholders, 28, 29, 29*f*

adoption continuum, stakeholders and, 28–29, 29*f*

affective learning domain, 13–14, 14*t*, 134, 134*t*, 145–146

analysis (A), in reimagined ADDIE, 15

"analyze," in cognitive learning domain, 144, 144*f*

Anderson, Lorin, 142–144, 144*f*

anticipated business needs, in business analysis strategy, 87

application of learning, specific strategies for evaluating, 160–162, 160*t*, 161*t*

"apply," in cognitive learning domain, 144, 144*f*

articulation, in psychomotor domain, 147

aspirational versus actualized culture, 39–43, 40*t*, 47

attitude. *See* affective learning domain

B

behavioral changes, and TD initiatives

    in evaluation framework, 115–116

    learning domains and, 13–14, 14*t*

    Think→Feel→Do Framework, 9–13, 10*f*, 10*t*, 11*t*, 12*t*

behaviorally anchored rating scales (BARS), 158, 159*t*

behaviorism, 11–12

beneficiaries, distinguishing from customers, 20

Bloom's Revised Taxonomy, 132–134

Bloom's Taxonomy of Cognition, 143

brand, organization's competitive advantage and, 35–36

Brandon Hall Group, 52

business acumen, developing of, 65–75

    business goals and course goals, 70–75, 72*f*, 73*f*, 74*f*, 75*f*

    knowledge of business and, 68–70

    language of business and, 65–68

business challenges, identifying of, 79–99

    articulating findings in language of business, 92–93, 92*t*

    business analysis strategy, 86–88

    collaborating with stakeholders to find root causes of symptoms, 82–88, 90*t*

reactive vs. proactive needs
assessment, 93–98, 93*t*, 94*t*, 96*t*,
97*f*, 97*t*, 98*t*, 99*t*
reframing thoughts about problems
as solution, 80–82, 80*t*, 82*t*
business challenges, transforming into
business goals, 99–107, 99*t*
communicating goals to learners,
106–107
determining if learning is appropriate
strategy for, 118–122, 120*f*
writing as SMART goals, 100–106,
102*t*, 103*t*, 104*t*, 105*t*

C

calibration, in gap analysis, 89, 90*t*
closed-ended items
evaluation guidelines and best
practices, 170–173, 170*t*, 172*f*
evaluation strategies and, 151, 155,
156–157, 160
cognitive learning domain, 13–14, 14*t*,
130, 132–134, 134*t*, 143–145, 144*f*
comparative business needs, in business
analysis strategy, 87
competitive advantage
external environment, 57–59
identifying of organization's, 59–62
internal environment, 56–57
ranking and understanding of
organization's, 34–37
compliance training, reimagining of TD
business model and, 49*t*, 50–51, 50*t*
complier stakeholders, 27–28, 29, 29*f*
compound items, avoiding in evaluation
instruments, 175
conditions of learners, instruction
objectives
content analysis, in ADDIE design
phase, 16
control, in sphere of control, 22–23, 22*f*
control groups, to evaluate results and
impacts, 162–163
convenience, competitive advantage
and, 60
cost leadership, competitive advantage
and, 60, 61
criteria, learning objectives and, 132, 132*t*

critical incident business needs, in
business analysis strategy, 87–88
culture, of organization. *See* aspirational
versus actualized culture
current events, competitive advantage
and, 58
customers
customer service and competitive
advantage, 60
distinguishing customers from
beneficiaries, 20

D

degree of proficiency instruments, skill
evaluation and, 158, 159*t*
demographic data, evaluation guidelines
and best practices, 169
descriptive analytics, in gap analysis, 90*t*,
91, 107
design (D), in reimagined ADDIE, 16
detractors, learner satisfaction and,
152–153, 153*t*
develop (D), in reimagined ADDIE, 16
development and enablement,
reimagining of TD business model
and, 50*t*, 54
diagnostic analysis strategy, to identify
business challenges, 88–91, 89*f*, 90
diagnostic analytics, in gap analysis,
90*t*, 91
dichotomous instruments, skill
evaluation and, 158, 158*t*
dichotomous items, avoiding in
evaluation instruments, 176
double negative items, avoiding in
evaluation instruments, 176
double-barred items, avoiding in
evaluation instruments, 175

E

economic conditions, competitive
advantage and, 58
elevator speeches, 44
enabling learning objectives, 132
environment of organization
scan of external, 57–59
scan of internal, 56–57

T

About the Author

 **Kristopher J. Newbauer, EdM, MHRM,** is the chief people officer and head of global people and talent for Rotary International and the Rotary Foundation, the world's oldest and largest humanitarian service-club organization.

Kris holds a bachelor of science in group social studies (secondary education) from Grand Valley State University, in Allendale, Michigan; a master of education in global human resource development from the University of Illinois Urbana-Champaign; and a master of human resource management from North Park University, in Chicago. He holds multiple certifications in both human resource management and human resource development, including:

- Senior professional in human resources (SPHR), by the HR Certification Institute
- Senior certified professional in human resources (SHRM-SCP), by the Society for Human Resource Management
- Certified professional in talent development (CPTD), by the Association for Talent Development
- Certified performance technologist (CPT), by the International Society for Performance Improvement
- Certified Prosci change management professional, by Prosci

Kris has completed multiple certificates in human resources from Cornell University and DePaul University. He served on the faculty of the Department of Education Policy, Organization, and Leadership in the College of Education at the University of Illinois Urbana-Champaign, as well as the Department of Literacy, Leadership, and Development in the Daniel L. Goodwin College of Education at Northeastern Illinois University, in Chicago, where he taught graduate courses in measurement and evaluation and organization development for several years.

He has served on the board of directors of the International Accreditors for Continuing Education and Training (IACET), a global accrediting body for training providers, since 2009. He served as president of the IACET Board for 2013–14 and was elected chair of the IACET Board for 2022–23.

Nominated by a former Rotary employee for his contributions to leading the way to extraordinary employee experience, Kris was recognized by *Crain's Chicago Business* as a Notable Leader in HR in 2020.

About ATD

The Association for Talent Development (ATD) is the world's largest association dedicated to those who develop talent in organizations. Serving a global community of members, customers, and international business partners in more than 100 countries, ATD champions the importance of learning and training by setting standards for the talent development profession.

Our customers and members work in public and private organizations in every industry sector. Since ATD was founded in 1943, the talent development field has expanded significantly to meet the needs of global businesses and emerging industries. Through the Talent Development Capability Model, education courses, certifications and credentials, memberships, industry-leading events, research, and publications, we help talent development professionals build their personal, professional, and organizational capabilities to meet new business demands with maximum impact and effectiveness.

One of the cornerstones of ATD's intellectual foundation, ATD Press offers insightful and practical information on talent development, training, and professional growth. ATD Press publications are written by industry thought leaders and offer anyone who works with adult learners the best practices, academic theory, and guidance necessary to move the profession forward.

We invite you to join our community. Learn more at **td.org**.